STORM HURLER

STORM HURLER

WHEN GOD HURLS A STORM AT YOU

RICK THOMAS

STORM HURLER:
When God Hurls a Storm at You

ISBN 978-1-966741-00-8

Rick Thomas

© 2025 Life Over Coffee

Edited by Sarah Hayhurst

Life Over Coffee
8595 Pelham Rd Ste 400 #406,
Greenville, SC 29615
LifeOverCoffee.com

Dedication

To Charlie, Jim, and Mark

This book represents my sermon notes from a series
of messages preached from the book of Jonah at
Fellowship Greenville in Greenville, SC. I have much
gratitude for Charlie Boyd, Jim Thompson, and Mark
Moody, who carefully exegeted and delivered God's
Word. I appreciate the Spirit's kind illumination to help
me write about what I heard. I pray the Lord will bless
you as you read these practical applications about a
racist, a storm, a big fish, a lost people group,
and God—the Storm Hurler.

For additional resources, visit
lifeovercoffee.com

Table of Contents

Introduction

Trouble is our constant companion as we navigate to that great city on the other side of our storms. Jonah was one such troubled soul. He represents all of us, a good but imperfect man—the only kind God will use. I am thankful the Lord placed his story in our Bible because I needed to know the terrible lengths the Lord would go to rescue and restore one of His children, while preparing him to cooperate with God in the grander work or redemption. I did not write this book as a detached author, as though Jonah's story has no connection with my life. The struggle of Jonah and the gospel-centered applications drawn from his story are not untested theories from an unaffected writer.

In April 1997, my brother's wife murdered him, shooting him five times as he lay between two cars in their garage. The judge gave her community service. There was no prison sentence because she had no prior record, and the courts determined the murder was involuntary manslaughter, which can earn the most lenient penalty permitted for that classification. It would be easy to be sinfully angry at her for what she did. I suppose I could say I was righteously angry, but the lines between righteous and unrighteous blur when the worst news comes. What I did know is that I needed release from the hurt that was harassing my soul. I felt as though I was drowning in the belly of darkness as the cords of confusion tightened around me.

It is easy to hate. Mercy is hard. I had to choose between simmering in my suffering or finding help through the incredible power of the Lord's gospel. Seething in pain was the straightforward path, but the long-term effects would be detrimental to my soul and relationships. I knew that. The more complicated path was to understand the point of the storm and then practicalize those purposes in my life. Part of the problem was a lack of mercy toward her, but God is a multitasker. There was more to my story. Focusing on the speck while not addressing the log would be a miscalculation of the worst kind (Matthew 7:3-5). Thus, I had to recalibrate, knowing that I could not change the problem, but I could change myself by the grace of God. The gospel had to become more than confessionally real to me. It had to become functionally active in my soul.

> And should not you have had mercy on your fellow
> servant, as I had mercy on you?
> (Matthew 18:33)

The gospel truth is explicit: what I have done to my Lord is far more severe than what anyone has done to me, and if God will forgive me all that I owe, I could have a heart of forgiveness toward others. The Lord gave me the grace to apply the gospel to my heart, releasing me from the pitfalls of hard-heartedness while positioning me in a place where I could help others, even those who are not like me. If you have a Ninevite in your life, I want to tell you a story. There was a man named Jonah. He hated a people group. God asked him to share His redeeming love with them, but Jonah resisted, rebelled, and ran from the call. He did not anticipate the terrible lengths that God would go to help him. He also did not discern God's grander purposes: there was something wrong with Jonah that had nothing to do with those he did not like.

The book of Jonah is really not about the prophet. It's

not about a people group needing the gospel. And it most certainly is not a big fish story. There is a transcending theme to this little book. It's about a relentless Redeemer who will use any means necessary to transform His children so they can maximize their usefulness in His world. If you want God to use you, it's vital that you understand the purpose of the storms in your life. It's not what you think. I hope you will be able to glean from this retelling of that familiar story.

1

A Reason to Love

The heart of the gospel is about loving difficult people. Jesus came to seek and save the lost. His death on the cross for undeserving people is the primary example that teaches us this grand imitate-able truth of loving our friends and foes well (Ephesians 5:1). Christ does not ask us to do things He is unwilling to do. He became the tested and sympathetic Savior, giving up His life for those who did not deserve such love (Hebrews 4:15), making Him the reason we should not forget this transformative aspect of our biblical heritage. It is also our responsibility to pursue those who rub us the wrong way.

Bless Them

Bless those who persecute you; bless and do not curse them. Rejoice with those who rejoice, weep with those who weep. Live in harmony with one another. Do not be haughty, but associate with the lowly. Never be wise in your own sight. Repay no one evil for evil, but give thought to do what is honorable in the sight of all. If possible, so far as it depends on you, live peaceably with all.

(Romans 12:14–18)

Paul, a direct disciple of Jesus, did not pull his perspective about interacting with people who do not rise to our "bless those who persecute you" cliché out of thin air so we could stick it to our rear bumpers. God inspired him to write those words that cut against the grain of proud hearts. Loving difficult people is the way of Jesus. Peter, another direct disciple, shares a similar but more acute thought about how to respond to difficult individuals. He had firsthand knowledge of how Christ dealt with sinful people. His evidence is overwhelming and should have a humbling effect on us. Listen to his sobering words.

For this is a gracious thing, when, mindful of God, one endures sorrows while suffering unjustly. For what credit is it if, when you sin and are beaten for it, you endure? But if when you do good and suffer for it you endure, this is a gracious thing in the sight of God. For to this you have been called, because Christ also suffered for you, leaving you an example, so that you might follow in his steps.

(1 Peter 2:19–21)

I Am Jonah

May I make this personal by extracting Peter and Paul's teaching from the old book and planting it in our modern hearts? Will you think about an annoying person in your life—someone who gets under your skin? What are your thoughts about them? How do you choose to associate with them? Would you rather avoid them or pursue them? Your responses will test your understanding of and faithfulness to the gospel—the redemptive work of Christ. God is a relentless pursuer whose goal for all Christians goes beyond our salvation. He wants us transformed into the likeness of His Son. I'm speaking of our maturity post-salvation.

Perhaps you have a spouse who challenges every fiber of your being when it comes to loving them like Jesus. Maybe one of your children has disappointed you one too many times; you have weak resistance, and your desire for redemptive parenting has waned. What about that church member who tempts you to sin each time you think of them? How about your extended family members? What about people groups in your culture? Gays? Abortionists? Democrats? Republicans? What about lazy people? Obese people? How about women drivers? You could clump all your annoying people into one broad category: people who do not do things your way. Wouldn't that be true? What if we invert the thought? How many people in your life agree with you, but you're annoyed with them? That is rare. Typically, the people who annoy us the most are those who do things differently from us. Regardless of who they are or what they do, God's call is the same: He wants us to partner with Him to carry the gospel to them.

> Now the word of the LORD came to Jonah the son of Amittai, saying, "Arise, go to Nineveh, that great city, and call out against it, for their evil has come up before me." But Jonah rose to flee to Tarshish from the presence of the LORD.
>
> (Jonah 1:1–3)

The primary purpose of the book of Jonah was God's call for him to go to a people group who were not like him and to tell them about the Lord. Their noticeable differences were their ethnicity and their religion: they were Ninevites. Jonah's problem would be similar to asking an American Christian to go to an Afghanistan Muslim to tell him about Jesus. When Jonah received the call from God to go to these people, he reacted by running in the opposite direction from where God was calling him to go. He went to Tarshish, like being in Columbus, OH, and God calls you to New York City, but you choose to run to Seattle, WA. Rather than going 500 miles northeast to Nineveh, he decided to go 2,300 miles west, in the opposite direction.

I Am a Runner

I find it difficult to be hard on Jonah because of this substantial log that projects from my eye, influencing how I think about my running friend (Matthew 7:3-5). Though God has not called me to go to an uncomfortable culture, He has called me to interact with uncomfortable people. How about you? The individual or demographic the Spirit of God has brought to your mind is likely your disappointing person or people group. It's that annoying person in your life that you would rather avoid than respond to redemptively. Jonah physically ran from the Lord, which is something you probably have not done. But I suspect, if you are like me, you have run from the Lord in your mind—a mental runner!

We do this by pretending the problems between us and the other person are not a big deal or that the person or the problem does not exist. The silent treatment is a classic example of this, treating the person as though they do not exist. Minimally, we can be mental runners who avoid challenging contexts or potential conflicts. Our culture calls it "fight or flight." I don't like this terminology because it lacks the gospel ingredients necessary to soften proud hearts. It would be better to say that we redeem or resist. The solution is not to pick a fight or run from the situation but to attempt to redeem an individual or a relationship—an act that would put God on display.

Of course, we could resist God by mentally running, but that's for futile minds. As someone anonymously said, "Trying to run from the presence of God is as futile as shoveling smoke with a rake." If Jonah had decided to redeem rather than run, he would have experienced great things with God. Though you may not be excited about entering a potential redemptive opportunity, God is, and He will not only be with you; He will help you succeed at what He has called you to do (Philippians 1:6). The type of mental running that we do happens because we forget that we are living in the presence of God, which is a severe doctrinal, amnestic mistake. After all, our omnipresent Lord is everywhere. "Where shall I go from your Spirit? Or where shall I flee from your presence" (Psalm 139:7)?

I Am a Pretender

And no creature is hidden from his sight, but all are naked and exposed to the eyes of him to whom we must give account.

(Hebrews 4:13)

Imagine if our theology were better than Jonah's because we have a full transcript of God's Word. Imagine being more aware of who the Lord is and how He works. How would this change the way we interact with others? How would this change how we think about others? We know that we cannot run from God, physically or mentally. God is with us. He is always there, persuading, appealing, wooing, and searching. At the moment of God's call on Jonah's life, none of this mattered to this marathon man. He acted as though he had theological amnesia. Minimally, his theology was not driving his actions. His sinful biases and preferences motivated him to run from God's clear directive. When I read the first chapter of Jonah, several questions popped into my mind. Perhaps you can work through these with me. Let this be your call to action for this chapter as you process God's call to do all that depends on you to live at peace with others (Romans 12:18).

- What is God calling you to do, specifically with a difficult person?
- What message from the Lord is clear to you, but you are physically or mentally running?
- How would a daily awareness of and sensitivity to God's Spirit living in you animate your thought life

and compel you to walk with Him—to change you?

- If you were keeping in step with the Spirit, rather than running from the Spirit's illuminations as He engages you with the Word, what would be different about your thinking? What about your life?
- How would your awareness of the indwelling Spirit impact the fantasies that tempt your mind?
- How would it affect a decision you know you should make?
- What area of your marriage is God calling you to change?
- What is the Lord asking you to do differently with your family?
- Is there a business decision you should make but are avoiding?
- How should you engage your neighbors differently?
- Is God calling you to better financial practices? If so, what is your plan?
- What would be different about living in a community with others if you kept in step with the Spirit?
- What about your angry or frustrated thoughts regarding God?
- Are there secret places in your mind known only to you and God?
- Do you live with a constant awareness that God is in all places at all times and has complete knowledge of all things, including the thoughts and intentions of your heart?

If Jonah knew anything close to what we know about God, he undoubtedly pretended as though he was ignorant of those things. He acted as though God did not exist. He was pressing the truth of God from his life (Romans 1:18). Imagine if he had a Bible like you and me. Think about all the sermons we've heard, read, discussed, and applied. How many blurbs have we "liked" on social media? How much of that dopamine courses through our veins daily? Yet, we can dismiss God as though He does not exist. No, we're not running to Seattle, but we can run while sitting still. We can run in our silence. I most certainly have done these things. I have been a pretender, though the foolishness of pretending does not change the truth that God is always there, and He is a relentless pursuer, especially of those who pretend to ignore Him.

God Is a Pursuer

> And he prayed to the LORD and said, "O LORD, is not this what I said when I was yet in my country? That is why I made haste to flee to Tarshish; for I knew that you are a gracious God and merciful, slow to anger and abounding in steadfast love, and relenting from disaster.
>
> (Jonah 4:2)

Jonah knew God was a relentless pursuer, which was part of the problem. He knew God might bless the Ninevites if he cooperated with the call. In the book's last chapter, we learn this through Jonah's painful but honest confession. Jonah's problem was far more profound than just running. He had hatred in his heart toward the people God was pursuing to redeem. But it gets worse. Jonah was criticizing God for being God. Jonah was doing all he could to withhold the grace of God from the Ninevites. Jonah knew that if he relented and did it God's way, the Lord might save the Ninevites, which was unacceptable. Rather than doing what God told him to do, he ran.

His response was a profound act of a man who is a prophet of God—a Christian. Imagine it! It should be sobering for us to take note of it and to examine our thoughts and motives regarding others. Is there someone or some people group in your life you hope would receive God's judgment rather than His forgiveness? Is there someone you would withhold God's grace from rather than extend God's grace to them? Maybe the problem is not about differences in personal preferences; perhaps the person you're considering has harmed you in some way. The question would be similar: Though they have done wrong to you, do you long to see the efficacious grace of God operating in their lives? Are you praying, hoping, and seeking ways in which you can be a messenger of this blessing to your offenders?

The irony in this story is that God's child was trying to run the furthest from God. All too often, this is the case. Religious people can be some of the most deceptive people. It is easy to hide under the shroud of religion while having a heart that actively works against God. This religious game is our temptation. We can create a wide gap between who we profess to be and the life we have. Jonah had a gap in his life that God revealed, and then the Lord called him to respond redemptively. A person God requests to do a complicated thing may want to run rather than pursue redemptive possibilities. Jonah ran because he did not have the heart of God, and the Lord wanted to expose Jonah's heart. The Lord knew Jonah had a blind spot. He desired to wake His prophet up and turn him around. Jonah had pockets of undiscernible disobedience, which would only manifest when challenged to respond to God. In this ironic sense, he was no different from the Ninevites.

- The Ninevites were living in sin. So was Jonah.
- The Ninevites needed to be exposed. So did Jonah.
- The Ninevites needed to be redeemed. So did Jonah.
- The Ninevites needed someone to call them out. So did Jonah.

Draw Near

Let us then with confidence draw near to the throne of grace, that we may receive mercy and find grace to help in time of need.

(Hebrews 4:16)

When we refuse to respond to the call of God to help another person, there are two people in need of help—us and the person God is asking us to help. The book of Jonah is not about the Ninevites. It is about God and His relationship with His prophet. The remainder of the book demonstrates that God is a relentless Redeemer and the lengths He will go to help His children love Him and love others (Matthew 22:36-40). If Jonah's temptation tempts you today, you are only a prayer away from God's lavish grace. God's call on our lives requires change because He wants to save us from ourselves.

He is not trying to ruin our lives by asking us to act redemptively toward others. The good Lord knows the more redemptive we are, the more we will have a heart like Him. We can stop. We can turn around. We can run back to God—if we are runners. The big idea in view here is biblical repentance. We can run boldly to the throne of grace, asking the Father for a fresh work of His grace in our lives. If you're a runner, stop pursuing hidden idolatries. Turn to Him in faith, and you will experience the redemptive activity He wants you to lavish on others.

Call to Action

1. I have asked many questions throughout this chapter. Will you go through them with a friend, asking God to reveal any hidden anger you might have toward someone?

2. Perhaps you're working with someone who struggles with a difficult person in their life. Will you use this chapter to help them see what may be unclear to them at this moment?

3. My appeal is that whether it's you or a friend who stands in need of God's lavish grace, there is no need to run to the next chapter before adequately reflecting on what you've just read.

2

Life in the Gap

Have you ever wondered how it is possible to believe the right things yet do the wrong things? It happens regularly—at least to me. I am in situations where I have the opportunity to do the right thing. Sometimes, I make the wrong choice in those moments—even when I know what the right decision should be. A wrong response creates a gap between what I know to do and what I actually do. My orthodoxy says one thing; my orthopraxy reveals another. If you are like me, there is a gap between what you know and what you do too.

Gap Dwellers

Do not be discouraged; you and I are not alone. The truth is that no Christian is perfect. We all live somewhere in the gap between what we know to be true and what we live out daily. It's a general hypocrisy, which is why judging another person uncharitably when they fail is wrongheaded. The awareness of our gap restrains us from judgmentalism. How can we judge others when we live in the gap? Thus, we never ask, "Is there a gap between what you believe and what you do?" We're smarter than that. Our questions are more intrusive, insightful, and clarifying. For example,

- How big is your gap?
- Is your gap widening?
- What are you doing about your gap?
- Who is aware of your gap?
- Are you seeking to close your gap?
- How often do you talk to God about your gap?
- How are you soliciting the help of friends to close your gap?

The issue is not so much about the gap, but rather which way we are going. Are we running to God or away from God? Tim Keller said, "Sin is running away from God, and grace is God's effort to pursue and intercept self-destructive behavior." God knew we would live somewhere in the gap, so He created grace for undeserving gap dwellers. Grace is His empowering favor appropriated for us. All we have to do is determine whether or not we will apply God's unmerited favor to close the distance between the person we are and who Christ is. What I am talking about here are confessional beliefs and functional beliefs: our orthodoxy and orthopraxy. I have used the term functional atheism to describe the concept of the unbelieving believer.

> Immediately the father of the child cried out and said, "I believe; help my unbelief!"
>
> (Mark 9:24)

Function vs. Confession

Functional beliefs ingrain themselves in us, guiding our perception, which primarily influences our behaviors. Our practical beliefs are who we are. These beliefs are the ones that put us in the gap. They are different from our confessional or core beliefs. Our confessional beliefs are what we have learned about God from His Bible. These beliefs are the perfect and pure truth. For example, a typical core or confessional belief is that God is good. The Bible is clear on who He is. No Christian would dispute the goodness of God. It is a core tenet of how the Bible talks about our Father.

> Good and upright is the LORD; therefore he instructs sinners in the way.
>
> (Psalm 25:8)

> For how great is his goodness, and how great his beauty!
>
> (Zechariah 9:17)

> And Jesus said to him, "Why do you call me good? No one is good except God alone."
>
> (Mark 10:18)

While we do not struggle with this confessional belief about the goodness of God, there are times when our confessional beliefs can be interrupted because of the grip our functional beliefs have on us. The most common occurrence is when we are not getting our way. How about you? When you find yourself at the intersection of God's story and your story, how strong is the pull to yield to your desires rather than His? Jonah was one such man. Though he was a good prophet who loved God, there was a particular situation in his life where he had to decide whether to cling to his confessional beliefs (who he knew God to be) or to his functional beliefs (what he wanted). Jonah chose the latter.

Function Over Confession

Now the word of the LORD came to Jonah the son of Amittai, saying, "Arise, go to Nineveh, that great city, and call out against it, for their evil has come up before me." But Jonah rose to flee to from the presence of the LORD.

(Jonah 1:1–3)

Rather than following God, Jonah ran the other way. I cannot fuss with Jonah too much here. I have done this a few times. A while ago, I was angry with my wife. At that moment, I felt the pressure Jonah felt. Will I trust and follow God by living out the pure Word of the Lord, or will I allow my functional—atheistic—beliefs, which are telling me to do things my way, rule the day? I, like Jonah, chose my desires over God's. At that moment, it did not matter what my confessional beliefs were because I was not yielding to the Word that I confessed. Truth does not matter if we are not going to live by it. If functional beliefs win out, we are no better off than an atheist because we act out functional atheism. Before you progress, will you take some time to reflect on a few situations where functional beliefs have overpowered the Word of God that you confess. Here are a few examples.

- I know lying is wrong, but if I am in a place where I may look bad, I may choose to lie rather than speak the truth.
- I know I should love my wife the way Christ loved the church, but I want to punish her through my anger when she displeases me.
- I know I should forgive others as Christ has forgiven me, but I want to make them pay for what they did when they hurt me.
- I know God looks at the heart and is not impressed

with this jar of clay, but I want to dress to impress others.

- I know looking twice at a woman is lust, but I enjoy the sleazy satisfaction of looking at women.
- I know I should obey my parents, but they are not perfect, and there are times when I judge them for this, which is why I disobey them.

Danger of Gap-Dwelling

How did you do? Will you speak with someone about your gap? You have one, and some things motivate you to hoist the functional flag of your life while lowering the confessional one you know to be true. Self-protection, self-preservation, and self-promotion are three hidden idolatries that will feed and fuel our functional beliefs. Our practical beliefs will often run under the radar of our behaviors. Part of what it means to live in the gap is to create a highly edited version of who we are for public consumption. We are not dumb enough to live according to the full scope of a functional belief system in the raw. We keep those things hidden, and the problem with hiding our functional beliefs from others is that we can believe our self-promoting efforts as we present ourselves to others.

It's self-deception. If we are believers, we want our functional beliefs exposed so we can change. We know we cannot live a lie, which is a form of insanity— an immersion in paranormal thinking. Para means alongside or outside of something. Paranormal thinking is beside normal thinking or outside of normal thinking. Normal thinking is biblical thinking. Sanity is living as close to biblical thought as you can get. Choosing to live continuously outside the clear and normative teaching of the Word of God will eventually lock us into insanity, and our consciences will soon follow our functional beliefs by hardening us in the gap.

I hope you do not want to stay in your gap, which should scare you to death. We have the Word of God and the Spirit of God, two means of grace given to us to help us change our functional beliefs until they are submitted to and guided by our confessional beliefs. If there is a disconnect between our functional and confessional beliefs, we must discern, decipher, and determine how to break the disconnect that keeps us stuck in the gap. It is a trap that requires extrication so we can be free to make the fame of God great in our world. Jonah's response to God seemed to say, "If I act like God is not there and act like God does not care, then eventually things will work out according to what I want." Though you may not have said such things, it is a standard appeal from the functional gods.

Fooling the Fool

> For the word of God is living and active, sharper than any two-edged sword, piercing to the division of soul and of spirit, of joints and of marrow, and discerning the thoughts and intentions of the heart. And no creature is hidden from his sight, but all are naked and exposed to the eyes of him to whom we must give account.
>
> (Hebrews 4:12–13)

Honestly, I have acted as though God does not see into the darkness of my heart. Even though God was telling me not to sin, I persisted in my way and did it anyway. I was pretending the truth of God's Word did not exist. I slavishly pushed God out of my mind by allowing my functional gods to shout my true confessional beliefs down, which freed me to sin. It did not matter what God's Word said. It did not matter what God knew about me at that moment. Functional beliefs can make noisy minds.

I want a life according to what I want. If I continue to hold onto my functional beliefs, I can get what I want, even if it means divorce. If I want something from someone and ignore what God says, I can use anger to get what I want.

—The Hardened Functional Believer

All Aboard

When you run from God, a ship will always be ready to take you where you want to go. If you harbor impure thoughts, eventually, there will be a bed for you to act out your passions. If you harbor self-pity and an "I deserve better" attitude, you will find the wrong solution for your sinful desires. When these things happen, you will affirm your evil desires. You may be surprised how often I have heard people justify their immoral behaviors through the signs they experienced. For example: "I felt horrible in my marriage, and though I was not looking for anyone, Biff came along. It was like we had known each other all our lives." And so, the unbiblical nonsense goes. Because she got what she wanted, she talked herself into believing God was in it. Jonah could have been like this too.

He ran from God, and guess what? A ship was ready to take him to Tarshish. My, my. Isn't God good? "If I disobey God and nothing bad happens, nothing bad will happen." You may disobey God, and nothing terrible may happen, but do not be so biblically naive as to think your actions are right or justified. A false peace can take you to hell. I have heard it said, "There is one thing worse than hell. It is going to hell while thinking you are going to heaven." Jonah got what he wanted, but what he wanted was not what God wanted. He was the fool whose deceitful desires fooled him. Just because we can sleep in a storm does not mean we are doing the right thing. Eventually, Jonah's problems worsened, and ours will, too, when our functional and confessional beliefs are at odds with each other.

From the time Jonah arose from his sleep, we see how all his functional beliefs were false. He may have dismissed God, but God did not dismiss him. He may have hoped not to get caught, but God was mercifully on his case. Jonah's functional beliefs said, "If I run, God won't care." Jonah's functional beliefs continued, "If I do what I want, God won't intervene." Be sure your sins will find you out.

> But Jonah had gone down into the inner part of the ship and had lain down and was fast asleep. So the captain came and said to him, "What do you mean, you sleeper? Arise, call out to your god! Perhaps the god will give a thought to us, that we may not perish."
>
> (Jonah 1:5–6)

Sin and Grace

God does care and will interject Himself at some point in our lives. Ironically, when the mariners woke up Jonah, he told them who his God was, which was his confessional belief, not theirs. His confession was what he believed, though what he believed was utterly different from what he was doing. Correct theology does not always lead to obedience. A proper confession of faith does not keep you from heading in the wrong direction. Jonah had functional beliefs opposing his confessional faith, which separated him from God. Are our lives a faithful picture of the implications of what we say we believe about God and the gospel? Are there areas in our lives where functional contradictions exist between what we say we believe and how we live?

> I haven't always lived up to my preaching, but I've never lowered my preaching to fit my living.
>
> —Vance Havner

There is only one way to close the gap between function and confession; we must return to our theology of sin and grace. We grow in narrowing the difference between our confessional and functional beliefs by cultivating an ongoing, deepening sense of sin and grace. We cannot ignore the evil or the grace in our lives. If we ignore the sin, we will not see it clearly, and we will not be able to appropriate God's grace to our sin. The central deception in the gap between functional and confessional beliefs is how we view sin and grace. As you probably already discerned, the only way a person will live in the gap is by being comfortably numb to their sin.

You can become comfortably numb by minimizing the sin. We do this by twisting, ignoring, re-labeling, justifying, rationalizing, alleviating, or blaming the sin away. Any of these responses will keep us in the illusion that all is well while we are still living in the gap. We must take our souls to task to snap out of the gap funk. The following tips will help you do just that if you take them to heart and enlist the help of a few good friends: the Spirit, His Word, and His children.

Call to Action

1. When you sin, you need to think more deeply about what you said and did than you may have ever done.
2. Then you need to ask God to reveal to you what you did or said and why you did and said it.
3. You must look under the sin by delving down into the real motives of your heart to understand why you did what you did. Behavioral sin always has a heart motive. While you should not go on a dismal, reflective, and morbid sin hunt, God calls you to repent of your sin, which is more than your behaviors. If you move too quickly to grace without

thinking about the heart issues that led to the sin, you cannot bring a satisfying conclusion to reduce your soul noise.

4. You must give the Spirit more opportunities to examine the runaway strategies of your heart. Jonah must sit down and provide substantial biblical thought about why he ran. It may have looked impulsive, but functional idols were feeding the engine of his mind long before he decided to run.

5. Without wallowing in your sin, you want to explicitly identify all the false beliefs that motivated you to sin. To do this, you must get some help from your friends.

6. As God gives you clarity, you need to spend time praising and thanking God for the gospel that saved you and keeps you from the destructive consequences of sin in your life.

7. I recommend you write a praise list, noting how God has rescued you. Thank Him audibly for His persevering grace in your life.

8. Share with your friends what you did, what God did, and how He rescued you from ongoing destructive behavior. Let the fame of God be known to others. By sharing, you will accomplish several things:

9. It will remind you of what God did.

10. It will motivate others to follow the path you are on.

11. It will make God's name great.

12. It will create accountability in your life as you share your story, which may keep you from running to Tarshish again.

3

When God
Hurls a Storm

What do you think about when a storm comes into your life? When things are dreadful, how do you wrestle through what's happening to you? Where does your mind go? I suppose most of us succumb to the temptation to focus more on the storm happening to us than the God of the storm. It makes sense: the storm is more real and nearer to us than the Creator of storms. God is out there, but the storm is right here, as our self-reliant spirit kicks in.

Lord of All Storms

The trouble appears more manageable than the God of the universe. Logic would say, "I have a better shot at fixing the storm than bending God toward my desires." The reasoning goes like this: "If I can manage my situation, it will be through my self-reliant efforts because I'm not sure God will cooperate with what I want, and He may not want what I want, the way I want it, when I want it." I recently counseled a lady in a not-so-delightful marriage. She has been in this marriage for nearly three decades. Her thoughts were predominately on how she had messed up and how her husband needed to change. Her thought processes were normal for people in bad marriages. Why not hope and pray your marriage partner will change?

It's not a wrong prayer. If he changes, she will get what she wants and be happy. However, what the Lord might want for both the husband and wife is missing in this line of reasoning. While it is wise to make sober assessments of how you may need to change or how your spouse needs to change, the more important thing to think about—the one thing that will steady your mind—is the Lord, who is in charge of the storm. While I affirmed my friend for carefully reviewing the sin patterns and how change needed to happen, I appealed to her to think more about her Heavenly Father, the Sovereign Ruler over all storms. It was hard for her to consider how God might be in her bad marriage. He seemed to be a distant Influencer at best.

Additionally, she believed her decision to marry, and all the ensuing trouble from that decision, was outside of God's ability to alter it. Though she did not say it this way, she did imply that she had made her bed and must now sleep in it. God was a distant bystander, and it was all her fault. She reasoned, "Because it was my fault, things will not change unless I figure it out and make the appropriate changes." I suggested that she re-prioritize who is really in charge of her mess. She may have made mistakes, but God is in control. His grace always overrules our messes. He is not just in our messes; He is super-attentive to them. He cares too much for us not to be in our messes, no matter how harsh our messes may be or who appears to be the cause of them.

Deep Love Of God

Do you understand the depth of God's love for you? I mean, really? Do you believe God may bring unremitting pain into your life because He loves you so much? Let me remind you of the gospel if you have trouble understanding this perspective. Carefully think through the Scripture below.

You could say these things happened because of the evil of men, and you would be correct. Like how my friend sees her situation: her life went bad because of the badness of her husband. She is correct.

> And they stripped him and put a scarlet robe on him, and twisting together a crown of thorns, they put it on his head and put a reed in his right hand. And kneeling before him, they mocked him, saying, "Hail, King of the Jews!" And they spit on him and took the reed and struck him on the head. And when they had mocked him, they stripped him of the robe and put his own clothes on him and led him away to crucify him.
>
> (Matthew 27:28–31)

Whether it was her sinful choices or her husband's, her life has gone wrong in many ways because of multiple influences. But there is another way to think about what is happening, using the gospel story as an illustration: God was orchestrating the gospel events, as the Gospel of Matthew reveals, for His glory and our benefit. We must juxtapose and interact with man's free moral will and God's sovereignty. Both are valid and practical in our lives. Somehow, man's free choices work within God's total control of everything. If we do not interact with these two truths simultaneously, we could quickly become an emotional shipwreck, especially when trouble comes into our lives.

> Yet it was the will of the LORD to crush him; he has put him to grief.
>
> (Isaiah 53:10)

God is in your mess just like He was in the crucifixion of His Son because you are important to Him. You're so important that He would orchestrate the crushing of His Son to save you. The Father loves you that much. He not only brought a storm into His Son's life, but He will also bring storms into your life. We do not serve a sloppy or haphazard God. He is an active God who gets into the details of our lives—even the sad details. He is in our business in ways beyond our understanding (Job 1:8).

> Look at the birds of the air: they neither sow nor reap nor gather into barns, and yet your heavenly Father feeds them. Are you not of more value than they?
>
> (Matthew 6:26)

The Storm Hurler

> But the LORD hurled a great wind upon the sea, and there was a mighty tempest on the sea, so that the ship threatened to break up.
>
> (Jonah 1:4)

Our thoughts about our troubles must be about God and what He wants to teach us through those troubles. There are many illustrations of this in the Word of God. Jonah is one such instance. God had called Jonah to do a job, but Jonah did not want to do the job. So, God hurled a great storm into Jonah's life. He hurled this storm because He loved Jonah and did not want him to continue living as he had. You know the story. The word hurled pictures a man throwing a spear at a target. God was hurling a storm at a target. In this case, the target was Jonah. He did this to get his attention. Here is the twofold sequence: God launches a storm into your life; God wants to get your attention.

Our first thought must not be to run like Jonah but to discern what the Father has for us. Perhaps you could say God sent the storm because Jonah was sinning. Okay. Sure. That would be correct, but you cannot say God only sends storms to those actively disobeying Him. He may love someone who is sinning enough to throw a storm at him like He loved Jonah. But we know the storm He sent into Job's life was not because Job was sinning (Job 1:1). We also know that the storm He sent into Joseph's life was not because Joseph was sinning (Genesis 37–50). And we certainly understand the Savior was not sinning when He went through His storm.

Attaching all storms to a person's sin can be dangerous, as though you will get a storm only when you sin. That is at the heart of legalism: "My performance determines how God will interact with me. If I'm good, God will give me favor. If I'm bad, God will hurl a storm at me." Not only is this poor theology, but it makes a sinful judgment about the gospel. It says our righteousness matters to God and lessens His judgment on Christ. Legalism is dangerous ground. We have no righteousness apart from that which Christ gave to us. It is His righteousness, not ours. If God dealt with us based on righteousness, we would get more than a storm. We would get hell.

Storms Save Us

It could be that God has brought a storm into your life for other purposes. Rather than determining whether you deserve the storm based on your performance, it would be better to ascertain what God wants to teach you. Work with objective data, not subjective or speculative thoughts centered on your desires, wishes, or fears. Here are a few sure things you know about God. They will serve you when things are going bad: He is good; He loves you immeasurably; His storms are for His glory, and His storms are for your good. You can bank on these things. Rather than getting angry at the storm or the person you think is perpetrating it, it would be better to huddle up with God and discern why He loves you this way.

If you do not keep your eye focused on the God of your storm, your heart will go to some dangerous places. If you think more about the horizontal realities in your life—the people who may be causing your suffering, your mind will trick you into sinful thinking. In Jonah's case, God hurled the storm at him because He needed to save Jonah from himself. Rest assured that if God has you in a storm, He somehow seeks to do redemptive work in your life. Creating a storm is one reason parents discipline children. The parent hopes the momentary suffering will warn and deter the child from continued self-destructive behavior. Don't you agree—parents discipline out of love? Though it is painful for a season, the reward can be eternal.

> For the moment all discipline seems painful rather than pleasant, but later it yields the peaceful fruit of righteousness to those who have been trained by it.
> (Hebrews 12:11)

> For this slight momentary affliction is preparing for us an eternal weight of glory beyond all comparison, as we look not to the things that are seen but to the things that are unseen. For the things that are seen are transient, but the things that are unseen are eternal.
> (2 Corinthians 4:17–18)

What's Up?

A discerning child will understand the storm is for their immediate and long-term benefit. If they are less about getting out of trouble and more about embracing the redemptive value of the storm, they will learn and mature because of it. God brought pain into Jonah's life because Jonah was running from God. To some degree, we are all running from God. Think deeply about your storm. How does God want you to change? I am asking you a redemptive question. Even through the storm, Jonah did not understand how God could bestow His grace on undeserving people. He did not want to carry God's redeeming message to the people of Nineveh.

So, God sent a storm into Jonah's life to rescue him from his sinful thinking. Sadly, Jonah did not get the whole redemptive meaning of his trouble. But God would not let go of His friend. He sent a big fish so Jonah could cool his jets for a few days. This second storm did the trick. Jonah got the message from His loving heavenly Father, and he repented. It would have been better if Jonah had sought the Lord when the storm first came, but he did not.

The first question we must ask when trouble comes is, "What does God want to do for me?" The personal redemptive purpose of our storms is the most critical question we can ask when trouble comes because God is always in our trouble for a good reason. It is more important to discern God before getting involved in the trouble that is happening. Here are some examples of wrong beliefs about God amidst a storm.

- If you believe God is not in your trouble, you will probably be discouraged or depressed. Trouble without God is a dangerous place to be. God is with you, even in your deepest trials.
- If you believe God punishes you, you will head down the black hole of guilt and fear. God's goodness to you should be your first and most sustaining thought when the storm comes.
- If you believe God is distant, you will seek to work out your problems without God. God was with Joseph, Job, Jonah, and Jesus. He is with you too.
- If you believe God is doing this because of your sin, you will have a distorted view of God. He is doing this because He loves you. Do not mock the gospel. The Father punished His Son for your sin, not you.

Fine Tuning

God sends storms into our lives to intercept self-destructive behavior. The key is whether or not we will let go of what God wants to change in us. It does not mean God will stop pursuing us if we do not want to change. When the storm came, Jonah refused to change. Then God sent a big fish, which gave Jonah more time to think about his situation. A large fish did the trick for him. When we run from God, expect Him to chase us down. He will not let us go without a stormy intervention. His love for us is so great and His grace is so immeasurable that He will pursue us even if He has to send a fish to get our attention.

A person in a storm is not entirely oblivious to what God could be up to with him. You may not know everything God is up to, but you will know part of what He is trying to teach you. My my married friend began to discern a few things God was working into her life through the storm. She had unresolved guilt, regret, bitterness, and anger issues. She also had a wrong view of God, pertaining to why the storm was happening. She did not see God in her storm, thinking her poor marriage was because of her regrettable decision to marry Biff. Poor theology created a relational distance between her and God. My appeal to her was to spend more time with God, thinking through these things.

The last thing she needed to be thinking is that God is not in her trouble. He is right in the center of it all, wanting to show Himself bigger than her problems. Having a God-centered view of trouble does not mean the problems will change. Her marriage may never change, but her perspective and experience with God must change. Who knows—as God begins to change her heart toward Him, she may be able to present a clearer representation of the Savior to her husband. Once she learns to die to herself, she may have a more redemptive effect on others, including her husband. Jonah became a minister of reconciliation when he stopped running from God. Isn't this the case with us?

Call to Action

Every storm God has brought into my life has resulted in personal transformation. Once I stopped running from how my heart needed change, my usefulness in God's work increased. How about you? Are you in a storm?

- What is God teaching you about yourself?
- What do you need to change?

Rather than getting angry or fearful at the storm, lean into God. Discern what He is teaching you. Experience His love while in your storm. If you do this, you will learn what Joseph, Job, Jonah, and Jesus learned—the redemptive value of storms. Who knows, maybe your storm will go away. Maybe not. But one thing is sure: God will change how you relate to Him and give you strength because of the storm He hurls at you. Paul said it this way:

> But he said to me, "My grace is sufficient for you, for my power is made perfect in weakness." Therefore I will boast all the more gladly of my weaknesses, so that the power of Christ may rest upon me. For the sake of Christ, then, I am content with weaknesses, insults, hardships, persecutions, and calamities. For when I am weak, then I am strong.
> (2 Corinthians 12:9–10)

When the storm hurler hurls the big one, stop and think deeply about what He is doing. He desires to remove all of you from yourself so your satiation and reliance are on Him completely. You will know when you have arrived. You will be a grateful person rather than an angry or complaining one. One of the characteristics of broken people, whom God strengthens, is their gratitude. Paul did not get a change of circumstance per his request. He got God instead, which empowered him to function despite his troubles. Through his weakness, God's strength was made perfect.

4

The Point of Your Trouble

How do you think about the trouble in your life? I counsel a lot of Christians who have a lot of adverse things happening to them. In a way, they are modern-day representations of Jonah—their difficulties are swallowing them up. One of the things I want to communicate to my friends in trouble is how they need a bigger vision of who God is, especially when life is stormy. Did you know that anything God does to you or allows to happen to you is because He loves you?

Storm Chaser

> And the LORD appointed a great fish to swallow up Jonah. And Jonah was in the belly of the fish three days and three nights.
>
> (Jonah 1:17)

Let us pretend you are in Sunday school, and your third-grade teacher tells you the story of Jonah and the whale. It sounds incredible, doesn't it? You go home and tell your mommy about the story of the man swallowed by a giant fish. Your mom tells you how great God is and what He can do. She also says Jonah was a Christian. You dismiss that he was a Christian since you already assumed it anyway. As a third grader, it does not connect with you that God would prepare trouble for one of His children. And it does not matter anyway. You believe in God, and there is nothing He cannot do. Besides, you are tucked away in your bunk bed with your favorite stuffed animal, and Mommy and Daddy are in the next room. It is a wonderful life.

> The waters closed in over me to take my life; the deep surrounded me; weeds were wrapped about my head at the roots of the mountains. I went down to the land whose bars closed upon me forever.
> (Jonah 2:5–6)

Now, let us step into your future. You are no longer eight years old or in a third-grade Sunday school class mesmerized by flannel boards. You are unhappily married and have been for what seems like an eternity. Your marriage has the feel of a prison sentence. You are daily drowning in the belly of hopelessness as the weeds of discouragement are wrapping around your head and the bars of bitterness are closing upon you. Nope, you are not in the third grade anymore, and this isn't Kansas either. Your safe little world where God was big and trouble was small has turned into a war between two worlds, and God seems distant.

What has changed? Has God changed? Have you changed? Is God still big, good, kind, and loving? How have your beliefs about God changed? How has your world changed you? Perhaps you are not in a stormy marriage. Maybe your storm is some other kind of relational tension. Regardless, the storm is not the main thing anyway. It is merely the context for God to show Himself strong, for you to show yourself weak, and for God to magnify Himself through your inability (2 Corinthians 4:7).

Laced Legalism

The storm has come, and Jonah is in a sea of trouble. Yahweh has appointed a great big fish to swallow him. There is nothing he can do. He is going down. He is going way down. Israel's relational and redeeming God appointed a fish to swallow this little man. Think about that for a moment. Our great and loving God willfully picked out a fish from the massive ocean to swallow one of His children. Maybe someone would interject and say it was because Jonah sinned. This diversion could be an attempt to protect God's reputation by getting Him off the hook. God is love. How could a loving God cause trouble? Be released: God will be okay. We do not have to protect His reputation.

But you do want to swim cautiously in those theological waters if you believe it was because Jonah sinned. You may get yourself entangled in doctrinal seaweed. If God did do it because Jonah sinned, then we're all candidates for fish food. We are just like Jonah—born in sin and guilty of sin. (See John 8:7; James 2:10.) We must not play the sin card too quickly. Sin is not the only reason God will take us down (or, in this case, swallow us up). It would be best to think more deeply and reflectively about what is happening in this story. The danger of assigning sin to Jonah's trouble can be an unintentional accusation against God's character. You may have heard something like this before: "Be careful. If you do that, God will get you."

Portraying God as a legalistic parent is a horrible thing to say about Him. It is shortsighted and does not consider His infinite love, mercy, patience, forbearance, grace, or the greater purposes He may be orchestrating in an individual's life. Job's friends made this mistake while missing the point that God had bigger fish to fry. Criticizing Job as a sinner is shallow thinking laced with legalism. Legalism says that God blesses or curses us based on our performance. Not only are the thoughts that God punishes us every time we sin uncharitable toward His character; if it were true, we all would have landed in hell long ago. Even our good works are stinking (Isaiah 64:6). Who can stand before a holy God? We must reflect deeper on God, our troubles, and how it relates to us.

Response to Trouble

For you cast me into the deep, into the heart of the seas, and the flood surrounded me; all your waves and your billows passed over me. Then I said, "I am driven away from your sight."

(Jonah 2:3–4)

Even though God prepared a big fat fish for Jonah, it did not diminish His great love for His servant one iota. If you are a Christian, there is no other way to think about God. You can never say there is a moment in your Christian life where God does not love you. There is an indisputable biblical tension here: God loves you and will prepare trouble for you. Somehow, our theology has to accommodate both of these things. If it does not, we will drown in despair and discouragement. There have been times when circumstances seemed to be closing in on me, and I was so discouraged that I had forgotten the core truth of God's love. Has there ever been a time when you thought maybe God did not love you and Christianity was not real?

At this point, I want to suggest something that may appear strikingly odd. What if you only had the stuff you were thankful for in the last forty-eight hours? Or what if God only gave you the things you have expressed gratitude for receiving? The purpose of my questions is diagnostic. It intends to measure the condition of your heart, particularly how you relate to God while living in a corrupt and discouraging world. Would you be characterized as a grateful person? Where would you be on the scale if grumbling was zero and gratitude was ten? One of the oddities of Christianity is the seemingly universal deficiency of grateful hearts. When you think about who you are and what you have, there should be an evident and authentic response of gratitude. Here is how Jonah said it:

> When my life was fainting away, I remembered the Lord, and my prayer came to you, into your holy temple. Those who pay regard to vain idols forsake their hope of steadfast love. But I with the voice of thanksgiving will sacrifice to you.
>
> (Jonah 2:7–9)

Thanksgiving Theology

God never decrees a humiliation for which there is not a corresponding exaltation.

—John Oswalt

It might be good to rewind the tape to remind yourself where Jonah was when he talked about his gratitude to God. He was in the belly of a big fat fish. Pretty cool, aye? Okay, maybe pretty cool is not the best way to say it. How about, "Pretty profound, aye?" When life is strangling you, what comes out of your mouth? After a few days in the belly of your trouble, how quickly do you regain your spiritual equilibrium so that praise, gratitude, and thanksgiving begin to flow out of your heart? It may be good to think about the gospel at this point. God decreed humiliation for His dear Son (Ephesians 1:3–10). But He did not do this without decreeing His exaltation (Philippians 2:8–9).

At some level of your confessional heart, you know God will correct all wrongs. You will overcome the evil in this world (John 16:33). You also know there is a divine purpose in the troubles He allows into your life (Genesis 50:20). The problem is not so much what you know (your confession). Still, the key is how you practically live out your theology (your function) when life is going haywire, and you cannot perceive God (Job 23:8–10). The problem with a thankless heart is that it reveals poor practical theology—how you think about and live out God in your daily life, and nothing will tell the truth about your heart better than being in deep water.

We can trust Him even when we can't trace Him.
—John Newton

Grounded Gratitude

If our thanksgiving is rooted in our experience, our gratitude will be the equivalent of a roller coaster ride. Some days, we will be up and grateful; on other days, we will be down and grumbling. If our gratitude is more about what we get or do not get, our gratitude will center on ourselves. Circumstance-centered gratitude is about the person. It asks, what have you done for me lately, God? If our difficulties do not govern our thanksgiving, our gratitude is God-centered. This practical application of the Doctrine of God (Theology) will steady us through any storm He brings our way. Give some props to our old friend Job here. Though he may have stumbled through forty-two chapters of unremitting difficulty, with a few mistakes along the way, he was not utterly out-of-step with the Lord.

And he said, "Naked I came from my mother's womb, and naked shall I return. The LORD gave, and the LORD has taken away; blessed be the name of the LORD." In all this Job did not sin or charge God with wrong.

(Job 1:22–23)

We see this at the beginning of the calamity God brought into his life. His eye was not on what God gave or took away from him. He focused his heart on the holy name of the Lord God. Genuine, biblical thanksgiving is more about who God is than what He has done for us. Our deepest and most authentic gratitude fixes itself on the character of God. Gratitude based solely on experience is like someone repenting because someone caught him. But if a person repents because he is ashamed and broken before a holy God, he has a repentance that leads to life (2 Corinthians 7:10).

It is probably not genuine if his repentance is more about changing his situational difficulty or gaining acceptance from his preferred people group. I am bringing repentance into this discussion because if we do not have authentic gratitude, especially when we are in trouble, we must repent right now. We must change. We see genuine gratitude and sincere repentance in Jonah's life. He was grateful to God while he was in the belly of a whale. And he repented to God even though his circumstances did not change: he still had to go to Nineveh. We cannot control our gratitude by our circumstances. Jonah was grateful while in the whale. Repentance cannot be a trick to change our circumstances. Jonah still had to do what God called him to do.

What's the Point?

> "But I with the voice of thanksgiving (gratitude) will sacrifice to you; what I have vowed I will pay (repentance). Salvation belongs to the LORD!" And the LORD spoke to the fish, and it vomited Jonah out upon the dry land.
>
> (Jonah 2:9–10)

The remedy for both gratitude and repentance is a grand vision and theological understanding of who God is. A more extensive view of God that has authentically affected our souls will make us genuinely grateful and ready to repent. The question for us is whether we adequately and theologically steward the trouble God has brought into our lives. As you see in the story of Jonah, there are at least two good reasons the fish swallowed him. His gratitude needed to be rooted in God, and his repentance needed to be rooted in God. If our troubles do not teach us how to be grateful and repent appropriately, we may be missing the point of our troubles.

Call to Action

1. Are you a grateful person when trouble comes into your life? What does your answer reveal about your theology? I'm not suggesting that gratitude should immediately manifest when problems arise, but we must quickly come to the place of being thankful for all things.

2. Is your repentance motivated by a desire to know God better or to change your circumstances? What does your answer reveal about your theology? The good Lord can see in the dark; if pragmatism is our motivation, it won't work. We must have genuine hearts oriented to God.

3. Based on this chapter, what is the primary point of your trouble, and how is that changing you? Perhaps you're unclear of all the Lord is doing in your life. Sometimes, discerning the mysteries of sovereignty and suffering can take years. But are you able to perceive parts of His ways in your trouble?

5

The Terrible Lengths of God

God's salvation is a gift that we must steward, though managing His salvation does not imply we can lose it—an impossible feat. But we must share it with others. Suppose we do not steward God's salvation by extending His gift to others. Who knows, God might go to extraordinary lengths to get our attention to motivate us to think differently about the gift. Jonah was one of God's children who refused to steward salvation well, and the Lord did go to terrible lengths to turn Jonah in the right direction.

Taking Care of Business

Jonah said salvation belongs to the Lord (Jonah 2:9). Yes, and amen! There is no doubt about it. Even though Jonah messed up, he was not entirely off his rocker regarding how he thought about God and His salvation. Salvation is God's, and He can choose to do with it what He wants, as we see with Jonah. And though he was a prophet, we do not want to dismiss his life as though it does not matter. Yes, he made a mistake, and his mistake made it into the canon of Scripture. Praise God for His grace. What if God dismissed us because we made a mistake? How awful!

What if you rejected someone because they did not

meet your expectations? Even more terrible. The mature Christian will find the good in a person's life and learn from it, which is why we can learn from our brother, Jonah. He said that salvation belongs to Yahweh, the covenant-keeping LORD God. Salvation is His, and if we receive it, there is no question it is an unearned gift (Ephesians 2:8). Though God's salvation is a gift, it becomes a stewardship responsibility for the followers. We are to manage God's salvation, a concept similar to other things in our lives since all things belong to God (Psalm 24:1–2). So, may I ask,

- What do you think about your salvation?
- Do you see it as a gift from the Lord?
- How do you steward this gift from God?

We have been trying to parent this stewardship idea in our children. For example, we have told them for years "their room" is not theirs. "Their toys" are not theirs either. Even more importantly, "their lives" do not belong to them. Everything belongs to God. He did not provide salvation for us to use in a self-centered, self-serving way, with no appreciation for, acknowledgment of, and responsibility toward the One who gave us all these gifts. You'll see a common cause of this theological breakdown in the person who "got saved so he would not have to go to hell." He wanted to "get his ticket punched," which is irresponsible salvation stewardship. It's stunning enough that he is not going to hell, but salvation is much more than a reservation in the celestial city.

The Rusty, the Glorious

Imagine at Christmas if a relative took your gift and was irresponsible with how they used it. Perhaps it may be okay to take liberties with what you do with some of the things you receive, but it would be wise to be more gracious, thoughtful, and responsible with how you steward God's gift of salvation. Jesus talked about prioritizing earthly and heavenly blessings when He distinguished between the rusty temporal and the glorious eternal. Temporal gifts and lasting gifts are different. The stakes are eternally higher regarding God's salvation. The comprehensiveness of the gift of salvation is staggering, and our responsibility regarding that gift is sobering. It is the most expensive gift you will ever steward because it belongs to the Lord. No earthly reward can compare to the unearned blessing of salvation.

> Do not lay up for yourselves treasures on earth, where moth and rust destroy and where thieves break in and steal, but lay up for yourselves treasures in heaven, where neither moth nor rust destroys and where thieves do not break in and steal.
>
> (Matthew 6:19–20)

One of the instructive ironies about Jonah's statement about "salvation belonging to the Lord" is the truth in which he spoke but the failure in how he lived out what he knew to be true. Jonah's confession (orthodoxy) and his function (orthopraxy) were at odds. This tension is fundamental for all of us. Our beliefs and our practices do not always line up. Though Jonah was spouting off about God's salvation— inside the whale's belly—it was not long before he was angry and defiant again after God resolved his problem with that big fish (Jonah 4:4). What he knew to be accurate and his desire to live out this knowledge did not connect after he exited the whale. Praise God for His grace; God makes wide borders of mercy for people like Jonah. He gives His children room to wobble.

If you do a poor job stewarding the Lord's salvation, you do not have to fret. He will help you to become a better steward. Warning: it would be a good idea to think about two of the ways He "helped" Jonah: (1) by hurling a storm at him and (2) by appointing a fish to swallow him. While my intent is not to scare you, it does elevate the seriousness of how God thinks about His salvation. It should also give us a different perspective on the trouble in our lives. Could there be a sovereign point to our troubles? Maybe the Lord, who owns our salvation, will go to unusual lengths to help us become better stewards of it. There is no doubt, according to the book of Jonah, that is what God was doing; He was allowing Jonah to learn how to manage salvation's gift.

Sovereignly Executing Salvation

Understanding how to manage the Lord's salvation means we must understand more about how God executes salvation sovereignly, which begins by understanding how God controls everything. There is nothing over which He does not exercise power, and nothing is outside His control. If He were not in control, He would cease to be God. Nothing can thwart His plans for us—not even our sins. We see God orchestrating His salvation throughout the book of Jonah. He is behind the scenes working to bring Jonah to complete repentance. There is no doubt that God is in charge.

- In 1:4, God hurled a mighty wind to help rescue Jonah.
- In 1:17, God appointed a great fish to swallow Jonah.
- In 4:6, God appointed a plant to come over Jonah.
- In 4:8, God appointed a wind to scorch Jonah.

While it is true the sailors threw Jonah into the sea, as we read in Jonah 1:15, Jonah gave us a sovereign perspective of God's work in his life in Jonah 2:3. These are what theologians call the primary and secondary causes. This theological insight is outstanding news. The Lord sovereignly executes salvation, using pagan men to accomplish His purposes.

We do not have a sloppy salvation. It is the Lord's salvation. We can manage our salvation with confidence, courage, and gratitude. No matter our situational difficulties, God is in control, always working for our good.

- **SECONDARY CAUSE:** "So they picked up Jonah and hurled him into the sea, and the sea ceased from its raging" (Jonah 1:15).
- **PRIMARY CAUSE:** "For you cast me into the deep, into the heart of the seas, and the flood surrounded me; all your waves and your billows passed over me" (Jonah 2:3).

Experience Temporary Salvation

God's salvation consists of past, present, and future components. In Ephesians 1:3–11, we know God was thinking about the execution of His salvation in eternity past. In Revelation 21:1, we get a sneak peek into our future salvation. There is also a temporal element to our salvation with our life on earth. The essential theological term for this is the "Ordo Salutis," which is the process of transformation into Christ-likeness. The Lord's salvation allows us to know and experience that (1) we have been saved, (2) we are being saved, and (3) we will be saved. Jonah was experiencing God's salvation in the temporal, as we see God rescuing (saving) him from repeated errors in judgment.

Though salvation has a definite regeneration effect—you are born again—it also means God will be "saving" us throughout our lives. He does this so we can further mature in Christ because we are not entirely mature at regeneration (1 Peter 2:2). This truth places a responsibility on us to respond to God so we can grow in our relationship with Him. This "requirement of relationship with God" will help us to change. Sometimes the requirements of a relationship mean God has to bring things into our lives to motivate us to improve, as He did with Jonah. Our daily changing is how we can experience the Lord's salvation today, in the temporal.

Understanding and applying this idea to our lives will motivate us to think differently about the trials in our lives. Our tests are not because God is against us. He is entirely on our side, but He wants to change us so we can more fully enjoy Him. At times the things He brings into our lives will challenge us to the core of our being. We see this throughout the Word of God—the Father allowing or bringing hardships into a person's life to further His rescue (redemption) of them. He needed to do some dicey things for Jonah, e.g., a storm and a whale.

- What is He allowing in your life?
- Are you maturing in Christlikeness or sinfully reacting to your storm or whale? How you steward your trouble will directly affect how you steward your salvation.

Extending Salvation Intentionally

I typically let the folks I counsel know that counseling's end goal is not for them to become better but for them to go and make disciples. A key component to anybody's salvation experience is intentionally extending it to others. There is an exportability factor to the Lord's salvation. He did not save us to live like a Dead Sea—a body of water with no outlet. Christ, our example, models this well. He left His place to come to us to change our lives. He wants us to do likewise (Matthew 28:19–20). Jonah did not do this. He did not extend God's salvation intentionally to others, which was the whole point of God speaking to him in the first place (Jonah 1:1–2). He did not want to share the Lord's salvation with the Ninevites.

- As a child of the covenant, are you calling others into a covenant life?
- How are you exporting the Lord's salvation to your spouse?
- How are you an agent of redemptive care for your children?
- How do your friends experience the Lord's salvation through you?

You cannot have a clear identity with God without living out the calling of God. Jonah had a lousy attitude toward the people who needed to experience the Lord's salvation. He was a poor steward of redemption. If you have a terrible attitude toward someone, you will not be a good steward of the Lord's salvation because you will not export it well to them. Suppose you try to separate your identity (who you are in Christ) from your calling (your responsibility to live out your identity). In that case, you will truncate your experience with God and hinder those who need to experience the Lord's salvation. To be a Christian is to act like a Christian. To do otherwise is "theological insanity," which is living counter to who you are or, to use the Bible's term, hypocrisy. Salvation is from the Lord, and He intends us to give it to others. What would hinder you from extending salvation to others?

- To your spouse?
- To your children?
- To your friends?
- To your world?

Part of our sanctification means if God rescues us, we are united to be with Him and on a mission with Him. We see this most prominently acted out in the gospel. If the gospel is about going, we must tell others about our salvation from the Lord. Jesus, whose name means Yahweh saves, is the ultimate example of a person who had a relationship with the Father and was an extension of the Father's desire to restore others through rescue. Jonah did not want to be an extension of the Lord's salvation. He mismanaged the gift the Father gave him. Rather than extending the good news to Nineveh, he ran toward Tarshish. God loved Jonah too much to let him mismanage His salvation. How about you? Which way are you running? Will you take some time this week to discuss this with a friend?

Call to Action

1. Why is it vital to steward the Lord's salvation?
2. How has suffering motivated you to be a better steward of God's salvation?
3. Have you thought God was punishing you because of your suffering? Why is this thinking wrong?
4. How you think about God and His acts in your life will affect how you relate to Him. Will you talk about how a wrong perspective on suffering could inhibit your relationship with God?
5. What is your practical response to these thoughts about Jonah's unwillingness to steward God's salvation well?
6. Will you highlight all the questions I have asked and write a few short blurbs about how you can practicalize these things in your life? If you're not a writer, will you talk to someone about these questions? Perhaps this would be a great discussion with a small group of friends.

6

God of Second Chances

God is a God of second chances. Have you ever heard that expression? It is one of those things we like to say about God. It is a Christian cliché that we cherish because we understand the need for and benefit of getting a second opportunity. We came into the world needing a second chance; God gave us the gospel: Christ died for our sins (Romans 5:12). Without a second shot, we would be eternally divorced from God, but the good news does not stop. After regeneration, we need repeated second chances, the beauty of confession and forgiveness (1 John 1:9).

Purpose to Failure

Jonah was a believer in God who needed a second chance. He was the Lord's prophet. It seems like he would have been more obedient to God, but he was not, which makes Jonah similar to the rest of us. No matter how hard we try to spread the fame of God's name, we will need God to be merciful to us. Repeatedly. We need second chances until heaven is our home and glorification is our condition. God gave Jonah an opportunity to trust Him. Jonah failed. God hurled a storm and, later, appointed a whale to get his attention. Finally, it worked. God was reorienting Jonah's thinking. Jonah's trouble was God's way of giving him multiple opportunities to respond the right way. Initially, Jonah rejected God's call on his life. Instead of going to Nineveh, he fled toward Tarshish. It is as different as heading west when you are supposed to go east.

Jonah was running from what he knew to be the right thing to do. God brought a big storm and a big fish into his life. I am unsure how long Jonah took to get a clue about what was happening, though his entire ordeal lasted three days. He eventually repented, and God had him spit out in the right direction (Jonah 2:9–3:3). The mindset motivating Jonah is probably no different from how the rest of us run from God. As you read Jonah's sequence of repentance, think about yourself and how God mercifully deals with you when you are stubborn. Does this pattern look familiar? It does for me. It would be better if I got a clue and listened to the Lord the first time so I would not have to go through all the repeated rigmarole.

1. Jonah rejected the word of the Lord (Jonah 1:1–3).
2. The Lord appointed trouble in response to Jonah's sin (Jonah 1:4, 17).
3. Jonah repented to the Lord (Jonah 2:1–9).
4. The Lord gave Jonah another opportunity, having him spit out (Jonah 2:10).
5. The Lord gave Jonah a second call (Jonah 3:1–2).
6. Jonah did what the Lord asked him to do (Jonah 3:3–4).

Gospel Engagement

I need second chances because I am a failure (Romans 3:12). The gospel declares me a human failure, and even after salvation, my imperfections are part of my life. I am not discouraged by my post-salvation condition because of the gospel. Unregenerate people are without hope, as well as Christians who do not understand the practical implications of the gospel. These folks do not understand or confront their problems appropriately. However, gospel people see their failures as opportunities for change; they understand the Christian's victory in Jesus. Gospel people can quickly recalibrate their hearts when they fail because they know God is a God of second chances. We have a second-chance gospel.

> Then the word of the LORD came to Jonah the second time.
>
> (Jonah 3:1)

Jonah did not seem to get hung up on the fact he was a failure. A proper understanding of the gospel can do that for you. Think about it. If the Lord would become a man and die on the cross to give you your first, second chance, do you think He would not complete what He had begun in you? It would be better to go ahead and get over the fact we are failures so that we can move on to God's redemptive purposes. You are a failure, and so am I. Chill out. I'm not speaking of a morbid introspection that throws you into despair, but rather of the reality of victors. It is morbid for people who do not understand the rules of gospel engagement, but for discerning Christians, the gospel keeps us from morbidly plunging into the depths of despair, or what some would call worm theology. We are optimistic because God is a finisher.

> And I am sure of this, that he who began a good work in you will bring it to completion at the day of Jesus Christ.
>
> (Philippians 1:6)

Damning Danger

For the weapons of our warfare are not of the flesh but have divine power to destroy strongholds. We destroy arguments and every lofty opinion raised against the knowledge of God, and take every thought captive to obey Christ.

(2 Corinthians 10:4–5)

You will find patterns of hopelessness in the thoughts of people who cannot progress past the mistakes they make. They get stuck looking inward rather than choosing to look upward. If an inward look continues, patterns will etch into their thinking, which can become strongholds. These strongholds will twist a person's thinking until they cannot ascertain and process the knowledge of God, as perceived through the gospel, which can give them the victory they crave. A person who refuses to embrace God's second chance will spiral into anti-gospel thought patterns. Here are a few of those anti-gospel dysfunctions.

- **GUILT:** I am wrong for what I did, and I am not sure God will forgive me.
- **CONDEMNATION:** I feel condemned all the time. I long to please God.
- **FEAR:** I am afraid of God's judgment. What is He going to do to me?
- **DESPAIR:** I will never get out of this trap.
- **SELF-PITY:** I am a horrible person. I cannot believe I did that.
- **FRUSTRATION:** This makes me so angry. I did it again and again.
- **ALLEVIATION:** What the heck? I am in a trap, so I will have some fun.
- **RATIONALIZATIONS:** Everybody does it, so what is the

big deal?
- **REJECTING GOD:** I am going to run from God.

Your Second Chance

I am unsure what happened in Jonah's mind other than realizing what he did, what it cost him, and his need to repent. It appears he did experience some of the things above, based on what he said (Jonah 2:1–9). His mind was mostly reoriented (he repented) to God, and when that happened, God had him spit out of the whale—sending him to Ninevah. Jonah received the mercy of a second chance, one of the underrated blessings of being a Christian. Maybe it is underrated because we do not fully live in the reality of what the gospel can do for us after we are born a second time. The freedom and power of the gospel can be obscure to us. This favor only comes to the humble heart (James 4:6), leading to a few relevant questions. How free are you to admit your failures? Can you talk to people about them?

> And when Jesus heard it, he said to them, "Those who are well have no need of a physician, but those who are sick. I came not to call the righteous, but sinners."
>
> (Mark 2:17)

There is an obstacle that will keep us from enjoying the second chance God will mercifully give to anyone who calls upon Him (Romans 10:13). We must admit we have a problem after being born again. Christ did not come for the righteous but for the unrighteous. There has to be an admittance of sickness to receive redemptive care. For the Christian to receive redemptive care, he must do the same thing as the unbeliever: admit his weaknesses, faults, and sins. The reason a person is unwilling to do this, whether a believer or not, is the same. It is self-righteousness—a high view of oneself, the ultimate grace killer. Christ helps broken people. The gospel is for those who are not striving for high self-esteem.

There is irony here. Though we do not want to make a mistake, it is through our mistakes that God can help us. This realization is not a license to sin so that we can enjoy more of the gospel. God forbid! (Romans 6:1–2). It is merely stating the obvious. We fail. God's restores, and through His restorative work, we are matured, and He is glorified. Grace comes to the lowly, not the exalted, which is why accepting the reality of our blunders is ultimately healthy for our psyches, while rejecting or refusing to admit the existence of our errors leads to mental instability. The honest and humble person will receive God's favor, as experienced through His redemptive grace. Nobody is as psychologically sound and stable as someone who admits sin and experiences restoration by the Sovereign Lord.

A Persevering God

There is still more irony regarding God's mercy to us: He gives us a second chance so He can use us. God is not finished with us just because we failed. Our second chances are often God's way of allowing us to have more significant usefulness in His redemptive purposes in His world. Think about this: you mess up and run the wrong way. God hurls a storm at you and appoints a big fish to swallow you. You repent, and God spits you out, spins you around, and now you are heading in the right direction. Do you believe this? It is an act of faith, you know. God called Jonah a second time to respond in faith, and he did. God did more than Jonah could have ever imagined, and more than what Jonah could do without Him.

What can God do for you and through you if you choose to experience the mercy of God through humble repentance? Do not become bogged down in the guilt of your failures;

see them as opportunities to turn to the Lord in faith. Then expect Him to do fantastic things for you and through you. Someone could ask, "Why didn't God get another prophet?" That is an excellent question. Jonah failed to be used by God to rescue Nineveh. Jonah chose to run the other way. But God persevered. He would not let go of Jonah. Maybe God was rescuing more than Nineveh. Could it be God was saving Jonah too? Have you ever wondered why God perseveres so long with you?

Sometimes, we can become so task-oriented that we forget the higher purposes of Lord's work. The story of Jonah was not just about the divine rescue of Nineveh. God is full of mercy—to His children and His enemies (Matthew 5:45). Part of God's mercy is to fix the wrongs we messed up the last time we were supposed to do right. The implication of this passage is as impressive as it is intrusive. God is digging into Jonah's heart while seeking to rescue Nineveh. What areas of your life is God calling you back to respond differently? Do you fully understand the redemptive care of God in your life? Can you think about the mission (Nineveh), what God is doing in you, and how His work might be more comprehensive than that mission?

Call to Action

> But I with the voice of thanksgiving will sacrifice to you; what I have vowed I will pay. Salvation belongs to the LORD!
>
> (Jonah 2:9)

Your sin does not disqualify you from the Christian life, a worldview that mocks the gospel: Christ died for all our past, present, and future sins. But you can sit in the belly of a fish for a long time if you want to ignore the God of second chances. It is up to you to follow through on those opportunities. You can have God spit you out of a whale and send you in a better direction, but you must own any sin that may be in your life, turn to God, and receive His free pardon. The implication of sin and the gospel is that we need second chances from a grace-giving provider.

1. Are you like Jonah? In what way? Please explain.
2. Are you resisting the Lord? If so, what specific ways are you doing this? Have you shared your struggle with a friend? If not, why not? What is the benefit of talking to a mature Christian, competent in God's Word?
3. Will you be like Jonah and turn from your idols? How do you repent? Do you have a sound working knowledge of repentance? If not, perhaps understanding how to change is your first call to action.
4. God was glorified through Jonah as Jonah responded to God a second time. Undoubtedly, the Lord brought Nineveh to repentance, but He chose to use His sinful prophet to bring about their repentance. God will use you if you accept the second chance He extends to you, which comes from His incredible mercy. Talk about a season in your life where God was a relentless pursuer and how He brought you to repentance. How does God's past mercy influence you to press into future grace?

7

Our Throne Addiction

A throne addiction is when a person refuses to allow God to be the King of their life; they will not relinquish their throne to the only rightful authority to our lives. The addict to the throne has fully bought into the first lie of Satan—you can be a god (Genesis 3:5). After the fall, humanity came with a pre-wired craving to a throne addiction. We call it total depravity, which is why we must be born a second time (John 3:7). The bad news is that becoming born again does not insulate us from the encroachments of a throne addiction.

Tenaciously Loyal

Salvation is a good start but not a total solution for a life on earth that wants to live well and spread God's fame. We are tenaciously loyal to ourselves and will fight vigorously, though mostly in subtle ways, to retain ownership of our thrones upon which we can prop our lives. One of the ways you will see the game of thrones acted out is when sin entangles someone. As odd as it may sound, being caught in or confronted for sin is not always enough to motivate a person to relinquish his perceived right to the throne of his life. Paul conveyed this tension when he wrote to the

Corinthians. Though he was calling them on the carpet for their sin, he was fully aware of the Corinthian's tenacious loyalty to themselves. He said it this way:

> For godly grief produces a repentance that leads to salvation without regret, whereas worldly grief produces death.
>
> (2 Corinthians 7:10)

Jonah was such a man who struggled with the tension of godly and worldly sorrow. The Corinthians, Jonah, and I are all similar. God gave Jonah a clear directive, but he refused to obey (Jonah 1:1–3). The Lord mercifully sent a storm into his life to get his attention (Jonah 1:4–16). To further punctuate the need for Jonah to come to his senses (Luke 15:17), the Lord prepared a big fish to swallow him (Jonah 1:17). After these three appointed events from the Lord, it seems like Jonah would have repented. It does appear he did turn from his foolishness (Jonah 2:1–10). However, as you continue the narrative, you see Jonah being spit out of a fish and booking it toward Nineveh.

Game of Thrones

But the questions are: has Jonah changed, and is he heading in the right direction? Let's see. When he finally gets to where God wants him to go, he utters one of the shortest calls to repentance in the Bible (Jonah 3:4). If you read the passage in context while factoring in how the other prophets typically blared out God's call to repentance to their demographic, Jonah did a poor job. He was broken, but not broken. He repented but did not repent, which raises two critical questions for us to ponder as we reflect on our acts of repentance. Is it possible to be grateful to God for rescuing us from our sins, but we do not change? Have you ever had a close call: God got your attention, but you drifted back to your old paths soon after the crisis? Jonah changed his behavior but did not change his mind about those nasty Ninevites. We know this because of what happened in chapter 4.

> But it displeased Jonah exceedingly, and he was angry. And he prayed to the LORD and said, "O LORD, is not this what I said when I was yet in my country? That is why I made haste to flee to Tarshish, for I knew that you are a gracious God and merciful, slow to anger and abounding in steadfast love, and relenting from disaster. Therefore now, O LORD, please take my life from me, for it is better for me to die than to live." And the LORD said, "Do you do well to be angry?"
>
> (Jonah 4:1–4)

As you read this passage, you sense the feeling that these are not the words of a man whom God successfully broke to the point where he had a heart for a pagan people or their city. I'm not suggesting we bash Jonah. How could I? I see myself in him. There have been many times in my life when God got my attention, but as the crisis abated, I reverted to my old paths. Repentance has to go much deeper than personal awareness of sin and our desire to be extricated from our problems. Perhaps you have heard the illustration regarding temporal repentance. It goes like this: The airplane was going down, and everyone onboard cried out to God. After the tragedy was averted, the people returned to their old ways. I am not bashing those airplane-confessing people either because I am like them too. The truth is, I can be a temporary repenter.

Deceptive Helplessness

In times of anguish and disappointment, our impulse is to reach out to God, but when the crisis ends, we climb back on our thrones. There can be a deception to helplessness that we all can play. This technique is not repentance but a mind game to gaslight the other side, hoping to avert discipline. It is a method of repenting to get what we want without a genuine heart change. This problem is even more complex when we think our repentance is sincere. If you have children, you likely have seen the deception of helplessness in action. When a child perceives the threat of personal suffering—the dad threatens to discipline them if they do not change—they can appear to be helpless and show a willingness to change.

They give you their most effective mopey face, a response learned through ill-motive and much practice, hoping you relent from disciplining them. Once the crisis is over, the child cautiously reverts to what they were doing before the storm showed up in their room. The stakes are higher as we age, and the consequences are more severe. It is no longer about manipulating our parents to get more play time or to get out of taking a bath. Adult throne games can have generational and even eternal consequences. Here are three scenarios where I have seen these games played:

- We mess up our marriage and do damage control but do not change.
- We blow it with our children and patch things but do not change.
- We get in trouble at work and get out of it but do not change.

Repentance Illustrated

Although Jonah did not have a heart change, God accomplished His purposes despite His prophet. Jonah arrived in Nineveh, gave an eight-word message (Jonah 3:4), and some of the most brutal people on the face of the earth repented. This passage is phenomenal. It would take three days for a person to cover the entire city of Nineveh. Jonah only went a day's journey and preached a short message. But his half-hearted efforts did not stop God. Jonah preached to the king of Nineveh with a more concise message than the most succinct social media blurb. The conviction from the Lord was so profound and compelling that the king was motivated to repent.

> So Jonah arose and went to Nineveh, according to the word of the LORD. Now Nineveh was an exceedingly great city, three days' journey in breadth. Jonah began to go into the city, going a day's journey.
> And he called out, "Yet forty days, and Nineveh shall be overthrown!" And the people of Nineveh believed God. They called for a fast and put on sackcloth, from the greatest of them to the least of them.
>
> (Jonah 3:3–5)

The contrast between what the Lord brought into Jonah's life and what He brought into the king's life is striking. Neither the wind, the waves, nor a whale could bring genuine repentance to Jonah, but the king barely caught a half-hearted, half-baked message from a half-broken prophet and was devastated by the Sovereign Lord. The king broke down and biblically repented, which should bring you hope. It is not true that you have to be devastated by a catastrophe to change. Jonah met destruction and did not repent as well as he should have. The king heard the equivalent of a whisper and was a broken man. God can be in the thunder (Job 26:14), and He can be in a still small voice (1 Kings 19:11–13). It is up to you to be a player or a repenter.

Get Off the Throne

The word reached the king of Nineveh, and he arose from his throne, removed his robe, covered himself with sackcloth, and sat in ashes.

(Jonah 3:6)

If you want to understand how repentance works, clarifying what the king of Nineveh did would be instructive. He was the king. He had a throne. A king sits on his throne. It is rare for a king to get off his throne in public. It is even more extraordinary that he would take off his robe in society. If that were not enough, it is shocking he would descend from his throne and sit in an ash heap. That is mind-boggling. It is impressive humility; it's biblical repentance. It is an echo of what we see in the story of the prodigal son. The king went further than personal repentance. He decreed that all the people and all the animals should repent too. Though animals cannot repent, the point is clear: the king was serious about repentance, as seen in the Bible's most extreme caricature of repentance.

I am no longer worthy to be called your son. Treat me as one of your hired servants.

(Luke 15:19)

Personal repentance should not be questionable. Everyone should perceive it in you. If your husband comes home in sackcloth, sits in an ash heap, and decrees that the dog, the cat, and the goldfish must repent, too, you are probably looking at a broken man. Unfortunately, too many times, we do not see radical repentance. We experience lukewarm apologies. Radical repentance will compel you to relinquish your throne by standing up from your throne, stepping off your throne, and sitting in ashes. Like the prodigal after him, the king did not want to stay on his throne any longer. He was for real. If he had refused to hear the Word from the Lord and had not repented, his life would have continued down a path of destruction. Staying on your throne is the path to ruin.

Repenting of Repentance

The first thing Jonah needed to do was repent of his repentance. Semi-repentance or half-hearted repentance is not repentance. This kind of repentance is damage control or image preservation, but not biblical repentance. One of the most common ways you will experience half-hearted repentance is in the expression, "I'm sorry." The wicked king is still on the throne when repentance is watered down to an apology. Let me illustrate. Biff sins against his wife, Mable; he gets angry at her. Mable is upset, and after an extended argument, Biff tells Mable he is sorry. Mable accepts his apology, and there is faux peace in the home. The problem with this scenario is there was no repentance. Biff did not step down from his throne. He, indeed, did not disrobe or sit in an ash heap. He smoothed things over.

In these types of repentance scenarios, the person rarely asks God for forgiveness (1 John 1:9). At best, it is watered-down, horizontal peace-making. Biff navigated his marriage back to its pre-existing condition. There is a temporary peace, but Biff does not change, and his marriage does not experience restoration. Mable is glad Biff is no longer yelling, and she is willing to accept the peace treaty over godly repentance. Biff will not step off his throne because he is addicted to his ego and desires. He also loves his image and reputation. The first thing he needs to do is repent of his repentance. If Biff does this, maybe God will change him. Biff's story is not about how the king thought about repentance. He took it seriously and pulled out all of the stops. He believed if he genuinely repented, maybe God would repent too. Perhaps God would turn His wrath away from him and his city.

Will God Repent?

Who knows? God may turn and relent and turn from his fierce anger, so that we may not perish.

(Jonah 3:9)

This text is fascinating. The king is saying God may turn, relent, turn. The Hebrew words are *shuv, naham, shuv.* Shuv is the picture word for repentance, but naham is the actual word for repentance. As we know, God's repentance is different from ours. God is holy. He does not sin to where He needs to repent of wrong actions, but He can change His mind. He does this all the time. It works like this: God decrees you will pay for [that sin] when you do it. If you repent, God will change His mind and not punish you. The text says God may turn, repent, and turn. The hope we see in this passage is the interaction between what people do and what God will do. When people turn from their evil way, God will repent of the evil He said He would bring them. When it comes to God's eternal decrees—His promise to keep His covenant—He will not relent or repent, but in some situations, God will change His mind. You see this clearly in Jeremiah.

If at any time I declare concerning a nation or a kingdom, that I will pluck up and break down and destroy it, and if that nation, concerning which I have spoken, turns from its evil, I will relent of the disaster that I intended to do to it. And if at any time I declare concerning a nation or a kingdom that I *will build and plant it, and if it does evil in my sight, not listening to my voice, then I will relent of the good that I had intended to do to it.*

(Jeremiah 18:7–10)

This concept is amazingly hopeful for us. God will not make us pay for our sins if we will genuinely repent. Though He is sovereign and in total control of all things, He responds to the choices people make, which can determine the direction history will take. An illustration of this was God's covenant promise to His people, the Israelites. He promised Abraham the land of Canaan. However, some of the people did not see that promise fulfilled because of the choices they made. God kept His sovereign promise, but human responsibility was allowed to factor into the course of history. God is the author of His sovereignty, meaning He is free to respond and interact with people's choices, but that does not alter the predetermined ends He has decreed.

The point of Jonah 3 is we serve an amazing God, and we should be impressed by Him. We live with the Sovereign God of the universe, who will bring all things to a predetermined end, yet He will change His mind if you repent. He is responsive to His people, and He always works in ways that are for our good and His glory. He will be receptive to you too. It is your choice. You can play the game of thrones or repent of your half-hearted repentance and do legitimate business with God. If you play a game, God will not change His mind. You will incur His disfavor. If you get up, step down, disrobe, sit in ashes, and ask the goldfish to repent, God will change His mind, and you will experience His amazing grace.

Call to Action

1. How have you played the game of thrones? Will you discuss this concept with a friend?
2. What strikes you about all the work that led to Jonah's repentance and the minimal work that led to the king's?
3. What does it mean to repent of your repentance before you can repent authentically?
4. Talk about a time when you had worldly sorrow but not godly sorrow.
5. What one thing will you do in response to what you have read?

8

God's Kindness, My Anger

Everybody loves to experience God's mercy when we behave poorly. The alternative is the Lord's corrective displeasure. When there is a crime, our impulse is to hope for something we don't deserve. Have you considered applying the same perspective for your enemies, those folks you dislike? "Blessing for me but not for thee," the cry of the spiteful heart. Perhaps this notion strikes you as odd, so I'll illustrate it with my friends, Biff and Mable.

Maturity's Pinnacle

Biff messed up his marriage. Later, he genuinely repented, and as you would expect, God forgave him. Now, he asked his wife, Mable, to forgive him. She was unwilling to accommodate. She was still angry at Biff. Then she said she had forgiven him, but it was not true. She used Christian speak to justify her attitude, but the proof was in her actions—she was not actively pursuing the reconciliation and restoration true forgiveness implies. The pinnacle of Christian maturity in a marriage is when the offended person not only forgives the offender but asks the offender if they can be part of the offender's restoration process. Think Christ here.

We sinned against the Father, Son, and the Holy Spirit. You and I were guilty. Because of the gospel, we had the privilege of repenting of our sins, and God released us from all guilt and condemnation (Romans 8:1). We, the accused, were made free, and the Father placed our deserved punishment on Christ. You and I committed the highest crime in the universe, but the offended chose to be part of our redemption. The story is even sweeter. We can now join the formerly offended Christ in the restorative work of the gospel. The offenders—you and I—can now cooperate with the offended (God) so other offenders can hear the same message that set us free. Amazing grace. (See Ephesians 5:1; 1 Peter 2:21.)

When Paul was Saul, he had Christians put to death because he hated them. Then Saul became a Christian and began to work with those he persecuted. His new friends were nervous about his conversion, but their faith in God was exemplary. They accepted the newly converted Paul and dedicated their lives to partner with him on God's gospel mission. Their response is what the gospel can do when we want what God wants more than what we want. Imagine if the offended Christians held on to their offenses against Paul. There is such a person in the Bible.

At Odds with God

Jonah was a man who struggled with joining God on the mission. It was hard for the prophet to praise God for His work, especially when the Lord's work brought change to people toward whom Jonah harbored a racist attitude. Isn't this how it goes when we will not let go of something? It is easy to interfere with the work of the Lord when our attitude toward others is evil. In these situations, we do not desire what God desires. What did Jonah want? He answered that question for us. Jonah did not want the Ninevites to receive God's favor. He did not like them and was displeased that they had turned to God.

But it displeased Jonah exceedingly, and he was angry.
(Jonah 4:1)

I am unsure if Jonah was fully aware of this, but his displeasure with God's work was a commentary about the God that he served. Jonah revealed his practical theology through his dissatisfaction with the Lord's actions. Sinful anger is a negative commentary about God and an accusation toward God. Sovereign Lord was the One who granted repentance. The king of Nineveh could not experience forgiveness unless God chose to forgive him. God showed favor to the king, but Jonah was displeased with what God did. A person who harbors anger while withholding God's redemptive purposes for others is at odds with God. The Lord became an obstacle in Jonah's mind because God was not cooperating with Jonah's desires. God was redemptively pursuing the Ninevites, while Jonah was rebelliously pursuing Tarshish.

Thinking Redemptively

Think about all the times you chose anger over redemptive purposes. Wasn't it for the same reasons as Jonah? Were you not getting what you wanted? If anger and redemption are our choices, Christians should always think redemptively first because we serve a redeeming, sovereign God. He is in control of all things, even the evil Ninevites. Our job is to pursue redemptive contexts and solutions while leaving wrath and judgment to the only one who can administrate such things righteously and justly. When we choose sinful anger over redemptive purposes, we are no different from the person sinning against us.

There is only one lawgiver and judge, he who is able to save and to destroy. But who are you to judge your neighbor?

(James 4:12)

> When [Christ] was reviled, he did not revile in
> return; when he suffered, he did not threaten, but
> continued entrusting himself to him who judges
> justly.
>
> (1 Peter 2:23)

Note how the same evil that characterized the Ninevites also described Jonah. The literal reading of Jonah 4:1 is, "It was evil to Jonah with a great evil, and it burned within him." The Ninevites were evil, and Jonah's sin was equivalent to their evil. The Hebrew writer wanted the readers not to miss the point. Perhaps your spouse has sinned against you. Did you respond in sinful anger? Though your spouse's sin was heinous against God, your sinful attitude against your spouse was just as appalling against God. Jonah is a mirror for the humble to see themselves clearly. Do you see yourself in Jonah? Biff needs a redemptive environment to continue to mature, which can happen if Mable thinks more about what God is doing to her husband rather than how she would like to punish him.

Sin Stratification

Mable needs to see how her sin against her husband is no different from his sin against her. "It was evil to Mable with a great evil and it burned within her." Who is going to stratify sin as though one sin is better than another person's sin? Wouldn't that be an odd conversation to have with the Lord? "Dear Jesus, I lied, but I never hurt anyone." Jonah had that conversation with the Lord, which implies his displeasure when juxtaposed with the gospel. There is a precedent for this kind of self-righteous attitude in the Scriptures. Notice how Luke talked about it.

> "God, I thank you that I am not like other men,
> extortioners, unjust, adulterers, or even like this tax

> collector. *I fast twice a week; I give tithes of all that
> I get."* . . . *For everyone who exalts himself will be
> humbled, but the one who humbles himself will be
> exalted.*
>
> (Luke 18:11–14)

You could try to make the consequential argument—my
sin is less damaging than his sin. That tactic would be self-
righteous posturing. I am sure the sin of the Ninevites caused
more damage than Jonah's sin, but the offense against God
is the same (Romans 1:29–31; James 2:10). The posturing
angry person seeks to justify his anger self-righteously
while still hoping to punish someone else because he does
not like them. For the record, we are all murderers: the
death of Christ was because of us. Self-righteous posturing
is an elevated view of self and a low view of God and His
gospel. Jonah had a greater-than/better-than attitude. The
bottom line was Jonah did not see himself as bad as the
Ninevites and was displeased with God.

God's Wrong Response

There can be moments in our lives when God's love seems
wasted. There can be moments in our lives when God's
power seems mishandled. There can be moments in our lives
when God's grace seems cheap. You will know if you're in a
Jonah trap if your displeasure with someone outweighs your
redemptive thoughts of them. Jonah would rather have seen
God's judgment fall on the Ninevites than see them restored.
At least he was honest with God about his sinful attitude. The
complexity is so profound in this passage: his honesty was
as striking as it was arrogant. We are on dangerous ground
when we are bold enough to tell God how we rationalize our
sins and are not making plans to change. Then, like Jonah,
we use sound theology to prove our points. Matter-of-factly,
Jonah tells God why he ran to Tarshish.

> O LORD, is not this what I said when I was yet in my country? That is why I made haste to flee to Tarshish; for I knew that you are a gracious God and merciful, slow to anger and abounding in steadfast love, and relenting from disaster. Therefore now, O LORD, please take my life from me, for it is better for me to die than to live
>
> (Jonah 4:2–3)

His decision to run was not impulsive. He made a reflective response, a pondered perspective. He did not equivocate with God. He knew what he did and understood why he did it. He did not play the devil-made-me-do-it card. He did not like those people and made no bones about it. Are we any different? Every time I get angry at my wife, I hear a voice in my head saying something like, "You better stop. You are a fool. Shut your mouth. You know better than this." And what do I do? I choose to continue in my anger. In that sin event, I do not want what God wants because I am displeased with her. This positioning is what Jonah was doing. If you were to stop him as he made his way to Tarshish and ask him why he was going to Tarshish, he would have told you, "I don't like those people, and I'm rebelling against God."

> [Jonah] said to [the mariners], "Pick me up and hurl me into the sea; then the sea will quiet down for you, for I know it is because of me that this great tempest has come upon you."
>
> (Jonah 1:12)

God in My Image

Knowing God as well as Jonah did was not motivating enough for him to stop sinning. You see this as you read how he talked to God about it (Jonah 4:2–3). Jonah's theology was compelling him to sin. He was right: God is gracious; God is merciful, slow to anger, and abounding in steadfast love, relenting from disaster. Have you ever thought about how the character and attributes of God could work against us as we ignorantly craft the Lord into an image to justify our desires? Every time we get angry, our sound theology is working against us. We choose our way over what we know to be God's way. We all know God can make a path when there seems to be no way, but sometimes, we do not want God to do that. We choose anger or displeasure. Our sinful choices rise up against what we know God can do.

If Mable would relent from her anger and begin cooperating with God in the restoration process, she would experience what Biff is experiencing—a deepening relationship with God. She knows God can do this for her, but she does not want it, at least not right now. She is choosing to defy her sound theology by holding onto her anger. She is heading into the thick weeds of sin. Jonah was already in the thick weeds (Jonah 2:5). Jonah wanted God to be like him and was frustrated because God would not budge. Jonah would not extend the grace he had received when it was time to give it to those he did not like. Though he was glad to receive mercy from the Lord, he wanted justice.

> You can tell when you made God in your image when it turns out He hates all the same people you do.
> —Anne Lamott

The Deep Love of God

"O LORD, please take my life from me, for it is better for me to die than to live." And the LORD said, "Do you do well to be angry?"

(Jonah 4:3–4)

- Jonah was not living out the grace he had received.
- Jonah was twisting the Scripture to rationalize his sin.
- Jonah was not going to be happy if God helped those people.
- Jonah would rather die than see them redeemed.

Jonah was so bothered by it all that he wanted to die, which should bring us to a choice. Will we continue to hold on to our displeasure against others, or will we pursue redemptive solutions? Will we choose spiritual death or spiritual life? If you are struggling with anger or bitterness toward someone, consider this as God's gentle, loving care for you. Even after all of Jonah's running, God was there to ask him a self-reflective question: do you have a good reason to be angry? Though Jonah was not persevering, God was steadfastly hanging with His prophet. God is a wonderful Counselor and a relentless Redeemer. The Lord was working on Jonah, trying to gently provoke his heart awake (Hebrews 4:12–13, 10:25).

God wanted to give him another opportunity to reflect, respond, repent, and rejoice. The same patient love the Lord showed Jonah was the same patient love Jonah should have been teaching the Ninevites. His response was to go outside the city, give God the silent treatment, and sit in his lean-to while remaining convinced that he was justified (Jonah 4:5). Jonah forgot that every day of his life depended on God's persevering love. Though we were made alive (regenerated), and God is sanctifying us, the fact is we are still living in bodies tempted by sin.

Even as the weeds of sin want to wrap around our hearts, the Spirit works in our lives. God is always operating inside His fallen creatures. He patiently works until He completes what He began (Philippians 1:6). What can you do if you're sulking in Jonah's lean-to? Take your displeasure to God. Do not run like the prophet. The solution is to go to Him and express your weaknesses—anger, bitterness, dissatisfaction, and unforgiveness—while seeking His tender mercies. Be honest. Admit you do not understand what He is up to and how He can work. Ask Him to rescue you from yourself. Become more convinced of what God wants than what you want. Let the story of Jonah be a redemptive example for you.

Call to Action

1. What is the irony in this part of Jonah's story?
2. Talk about a time when you were living in a similar irony.
3. What is the solution for a self-righteous person? How would you help them?
4. What does it mean that God is a persevering God? Talk about a time when God persevered and pursued you, leading you to repentance.

9

Caring for the Clueless

Let us go ahead and level the playing field: we are all clueless to some degree. We all need help. We all need grace. It does not matter your demographic; we need God's mercy. We are grace-dependent creatures, which is a cross-elevating, ground-leveling truth that motivates us never to judge anyone uncharitably. Perhaps a few illustrations about this universal clueless problem would be helpful.

All Are Clueless

- **HUSBANDS:** When I get angry at my wife, I have a theologically detached moment (TDM). I am momentarily clueless. I need God's intervention to bring me back to a right mind.
- **WIVES:** When a wife nags or disrespects her husband, she needs God's redemptive mercies. Though he may have done wrong, she is clueless regarding her scope and responsibility to help him.
- **CHILDREN:** We know they are clueless. We understand their need for patience, long-suffering, forbearance, and practical leadership to guide them into adulthood.
- **UNBELIEVERS:** How about the unregenerate individual?

Does he fully comprehend his offense against God? Spiritual ignorance is his condition, and grace is his need.

- **REGENERATE:** Even those who have been born again do not fully understand the depth of their need for daily grace and mercy (1 John 1:7–10).

My list is not an exhortation to let people off the hook so that they do not have to be held accountable for their actions. It's an admission of truth: we are unaware of God's completed mind and unable to do what He can do. We need help. We can be clueless, necessitating God's intervening mercy. You see our cluelessness in the words of the Savior as He was dying on the cross. I am sure the people of that day felt assured of what they were doing. Not so, from God's perspective; they were woefully clueless and needed Him more than they imagined.

> And Jesus said, "Father, forgive them, for they know not what they do."
>
> (Luke 23:34)

Clueless in Nineveh

> And should not I pity Nineveh, that great city, in which there are more than 120,000 persons who do not know their right hand from their left, and also much cattle?
>
> (Jonah 4:11)

Cluelessness is the point that we have reached in our study of Jonah. The last verse of the book provides the key to the whole book while appealing to Jonah and us. Because Jonah did not answer the Lord's question—the book ended abruptly—the query is left dangling at the end of a short story about a hard-hearted and racist man. We are left to speculate about how Jonah answered the question. We can also assume and apply the question to ourselves. How would you answer it: Should the Lord pity the clueless? Should the Lord pity you? The context of the book and the exegetical implication of this verse seem to say the Ninevites were clueless people. They did not fully understand what they were doing and needed the Lord's intervention.

If you read the whole book in one sitting while trying to understand the point, it appears the Lord wanted to help the ignorant Ninevites, and He was using a clueless man to carry His message to clueless people. The Lord said the Ninevites did not know their right hand from their left hand. The Lord had been appealing to Jonah to participate in His redemptive rescue of these wayward and blind people. From the first two verses of the book, the Lord was considering these people and their need for Him to intervene in their lives. We see God as a relentless, grace-giving, mercy-offering Redeemer from the beginning to the end. Jonah is a self-centered and angry prophet who would rather die than see the blind Ninevites enjoying the grace of God. He wants them to stay clueless and lost.

> Now the word of the LORD came to Jonah the son of Amittai, saying, "Arise, go to Nineveh, that great city, and call out against it, for their evil has come up before me."
>
> (Jonah 1:1–2)

A Relentless Redeemer

Jonah did not want to live in a world that extends grace to his enemies (Jonah 4:3). What was implied in the first three chapters is said explicitly in chapter 4. God comes as the wonderful Counselor and the relentless Redeemer, asking Jonah some challenging questions (Jonah 4:4). Jonah did not like his question-asking God, so he left the scene to sit under a shelter. He hoped to take a wait-and-see attitude toward the Ninevites. There is no question about what he was hoping for: it was not pity, mercy, or grace. The gospel irony in this passage is that the Lord was showing the same mercy to Jonah that He was offering to the Ninevites. God was not just a relentless Redeemer for the Ninevites. They were not the only clueless people who needed His help.

I will have mercy on whom I have mercy, and I will have compassion on whom I have compassion.
(Romans 9:15)

God would not let the Ninevites go, and He was not about to let go of His prophet. Even when you run from God, He runs hard after you. Even when you give up on God, He will not give up on you. God's grace is the only thing in this story that is more shocking than Jonah's sin. Nobody will be as patient and kind to you as God will. No matter what your sin is, God's grace is greater still. Jonah blows off God's question and leaves the scene. But his sinful action does not deter God; He comes back to him another way—He gives Jonah a plant to make him happy (Jonah 4:6). Jonah seems to have it made in the shade. Then God comes right back and takes away the plant. Jonah loses his comfort and his cool; he wants to die. Again (Jonah 4:8).

Ignoring God

And the LORD said, "Do you do well to be angry?"
(Jonah 4:4)

Initially, God appointed a storm and a whale to get Jonah's attention. Though it was a wake-up call, it did not wake him up. In this passage, God appoints a plant and a worm to get the prophet's attention. Jonah was happy with his plant, and things were going well. When the worm came along, Jonah was back to being mad. Jonah did not seem to understand how God used the plant and the worm to draw out his anger. The Lord was turning up the heat, using one of His tiniest creations. Do you see what was happening to Jonah? He was an angry man. The longer he resisted God, the more upset he became. Even the little discomforts of life were becoming significant annoyances. When you continue to resist God, you will continue down a self-destructive path to where anything and everything will cause you anger. Take note of Jonah's sinful progression:

- God gave Jonah a plant. Jonah was happy–verse 6.
- God appointed a worm for Jonah. Jonah was unhappy–verse 7.
- God sent an east wind to Jonah. Jonah wanted to die–verse 8.

Do you see the progression of sin for the angry man? What are we talking about here—weeds, worms, and wind? Jonah was coming unglued. He was a mess. The most minor things were setting him off in anger. This problem was not so much about the Ninevites anymore as it was about Jonah's worship dysfunction. It is as though the Lord was saying, "You are the cause of your misery." God kept asking Jonah questions. He wanted Jonah to see how this was not primarily about pagan people getting saved. Jonah could whine and whine about the Ninevites, but he was missing the point. If a man goes from being angry at a people group to angry at worms and plants, I think we can safely conclude he is an angry man.

> But God said to Jonah, "Do you do well to be angry for the plant?"
>
> (Jonah 4:9)

Jonah was the cause of his misery. His anger was not primarily about what was happening in his external world but about what was happening inside him. Our anger is the same. When we go from anger over big things to anger over little things, we have bigger problems than we realize. These little annoyances are God's small ways of teaching us about His extravagant grace. Isn't this how most arguments go? We get angry at a traffic light, not realizing our anger hurts our spouses, children, and possibly other motorists, not to mention defaming God's name.

Misplaced Affections

We get angry over spilled milk, and our children are left to absorb the mess of our sins. We lose a paper due to a software malfunction, and three people are on the receiving end of our sin. Our spouses disappoint us again, and we let them have it—and we are only talking about a minor infraction. A husband says something unkind, but at that moment, the heat of his words negates the redemptive possibility the wife could exhibit. What I am identifying is the jostling of our comfort, which was Jonah's problem. An entire people group was going to hell, and Jonah was worried about his happiness in his lean-to. A significant difference between how we can love and how God loves is that He will always value people over personal comfort. Worms and plants are not the objects of His affection, but they can be ours.

Claiming to be wise, they became fools, and exchanged the glory of the immortal God for images resembling mortal man and birds and animals and creeping things.

(Romans 1:22–23)

Here are a few plants and worms that can get in the way of our affection for people. These things can mean the most to us, even sinning against God and others when something rattles our idols: reputation, convenience, health, preferences, materialism, and appearance. Augustine said, "The city of God is a place where the inhabitants love people and walk on gold. The city of man is a place where the inhabitants love gold and walk on people." The entire book of Jonah comes down to this final question. If Jonah cared so much about a plant he had nothing to do with, shouldn't God care about a lost and hell-bound city of people?

And the LORD said, "You pity the plant, for which you did not labor, nor did you make it grow, which came into being in a night and perished in a night. And should not I pity Nineveh, that great city, in which there are more than 120,000 persons who do not know their right hand from their left, and also much cattle?"

(Jonah 4:10–11)

Nineveh Is Clueless

They have gone astray. They have lost their way. Without God, they have no idea what living for Him or each other means. The book stops with an open-ended question. We do not know how Jonah answered this query, but the open nature of the question leaves us with a similar appeal. Shouldn't I care about the people who appear to be enemies of God? Let's get personal. Are you okay with the fact that God passionately cares for and wants to show grace to people you cannot stand? How God interacts with Jonah seems to indicate how the presence of enemies in his life is not random. God was inviting the prophet into a deeper understanding and experience of His grace. God, the question-asker, was exploring Jonah's heart, helping him to understand how the enemies of God could be used redemptively in his life. Perhaps a few well-placed questions would benefit us at this juncture.

- Who is the toxic person in your life?
- Who is the annoying person in your life?
- Who is the adversarial person in your life?
- Who is the evil person in your life?

Be careful how you think about them. If you focus more on what they did and who they are, your starting place is wrong. The Ninevites consumed Jonah's mental state to the point where he could not see himself. If our first thought is what they have done to us rather than what we have done to Christ, we will not be able to think and act redemptively toward them—especially at the moment when we need to respond redemptively. This backward thinking is what happened to Jonah. He could clearly tell you what was wrong with the Ninevites, but he seemed to have amnesia regarding how he saw himself. If the gospel were actively guarding his heart and mind, he would have begun redemptively rather than reactively.

Years ago, I asked a lady how her husband had failed her. She met this first question with a list that went on for about five minutes. When she finished, I asked her to tell me how she had failed her husband. She met my second question with a perplexed and blank stare. She went from articulate to amnesia in a matter of seconds. If this is how we think about others, especially those who have hurt us, redemption is not our goal. The gospel is not the primary thing in our lives. Maybe your enemies are not obstacles to keep you from growing in grace but a means by which you can grow in grace. You will know if they are obstacles by how you think about and respond to them.

1. Jonah focused on the Ninevites' sin.
2. God focused on the Ninevites' need for mercy.
3. What is your focus regarding the clueless?

Call to Action

Sometimes, our enemies are God's instruments of grace to draw out who we are and what is wrong with us. Your enemy could be the most clarifying mirror for the brokenness in your soul.

1. If God's grace is unconditionally extended to His enemies as He brings it to you, how should you think about God, your enemies, and yourself?
2. Are you okay with God wanting to use your enemy to change you? The clueless need your help, not your scorn. If they do not get God's mercy and grace, they will pay for their sins one way or the other.
3. Astonishingly, God would allow us to be part of His redemptive work. How does this statement affect you? What changes, if any, do you need to make? Will you talk to someone about these things?

About the Author

 Rick Thomas launched the Life Over Coffee global training network in 2008 to bring hope and help for you and others by creating resources that spark conversations for transformation. His primary responsibilities are resource creation and leadership development, which he does through speaking, writing, podcasting, and educating. In 1990 he earned a BA in Theology and, in 1991, a BS in Education. In 1993, he received his ordination into Christian ministry, and in 2000, he graduated with an MA in Counseling from The Master's University. In 2006, he was recognized as a Fellow of the Association of Certified Biblical Counselors (ACBC).

Other Books Available from
Life Over Coffee

Boasting in Weakness
Centering Your Marriage on Christ
Communication
Complete Marriage
Don't Apologize
Exchange the Truth for a Lie
Help My Marriage Has Grown Cold
Identity Crisis
Local Church
Loving Me
Mad
Marriage Devotion We Are One
Politics and Culture
Parenting Devotion from Zero to Adulthood
Sex, Temptation, and Modesty
Storm Hurler
The Cyber Effect
The Talk
Wives Leading
You Decide